LEARNING RESOURCES CTR/NEW ENGLAND TECH.
GEN   HD58.8.K68 1989
Kovach, Barb   The organizational gameboa

3 0147 0001 4298 7

Y0-BQG-354

HD 58.8 .K68 1989

Kovach, Barbara E.

The organizatio   ard

DATE DUE

D

The
Organizational
Gameboard

Winning the
Game at Work
in Changing Times

NEW ENGLAND INSTITUTE
OF TECHNOLOGY
LEARNING RESOURCES CENTER

The Organizational Gameboard

Winning the Game at Work in Changing Times

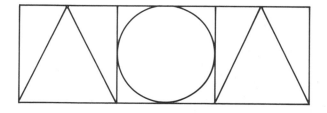

Barbara E. Kovach, Ph.D.
Director, Leadership Development Institute
Rutgers University

Educational Technology Publications
Englewood Cliffs, New Jersey 07632

NEW ENGLAND INSTITUTE
OF TECHNOLOGY
LEARNING RESOURCES CENTER

18741159

Library of Congress Cataloging in Publication Data

Kovach, Barbara E.
    The organizational gameboard.

    Bibliography: p.
    Includes index.
    1. Organizational change. 2. Communication in
organization. 3. Organizational effectiveness.
I. Title.
HD58.8.K68 1989   650.1   88-31070
ISBN 0-87778-215-6

Copyright © 1989 Educational Technology Publications, Inc., Englewood Cliffs, New Jersey 07632. All
rights reserved. No part of this book may be
reproduced or transmitted, in any form or by any
means, electronic or mechanical, including photo-
copying, recording, or by any information storage
and retrieval system, without permission in writing
from the Publisher.

Printed in the United States of America.

Library of Congress Catalog Card Number:
88-31070.

International Standard Book Number:
0-87778-215-6.

First Printing: January, 1989.

PREFACE

Almost all of us are players on an organizational gameboard. We enter the game at "start" and move - with ease or difficulty - toward the middle of the board, some of us actually approaching "finish." The gameboard is the business, governmental or educational setting in which we work each day. The rules are all those expectations about our behavior which are held by ourselves and the others on the gameboard. Whether or not we know the rules, and how we play by these rules, determines our success in playing the game.

Most of our problems in the course of the game come from a misunderstanding of the rules. We do not see that *this* is expected and *that* is not, that *this* event sets in motion the patterns leading to *that* event. There are reasons for our misunderstanding: first, almost all of the rules by which we play the game are never written down, never spelled out, and exist only in the minds of those who evaluate and support us; second, the sets of rules by which we play the game have been changing very rapidly in the last fifteen years so that it becomes important to *know* the rules and to *know how to learn* new rules and new forms of the old ones. Players who do not understand the rules, today, are often swept off the gameboard. Organizations with many such players will not survive.

From the late 1940s through the early 1970s, economic conditions in America were relatively stable. Today was not too different from yesterday and those at work were able to slowly learn the rules of the game over time - *without knowing that they were doing so.* By watching and listening to those around them, with occasionally coaching and mentoring from bosses and mentors, players on the organizational gameboards of this era were able to learn what it was they were to do, how they were to behave, and what it took to win the game. They did not know this consciously, rather they assumed that this was just the way things were. Players assumed that these rules defined the unchanging contexts of the games which they played.

Since the mid-1970s, however, the American economy has grown increasingly turbulent and today does not bear much resemblance to yesterday. On the organizational gameboard of our era, we cannot afford to learn the rules slowly and without knowing that we do so; rather, we must learn the rules quickly and be able to change and follow other sets of rules at any given moment. In order to learn more than one set of rules and be able to shift from one set to another, we must know that the rules are indeed rules (however unspoken and unstated) and we must know how to learn variations on these rules as we move through changing environments. So we must make rule-learning a conscious activity, we must become aware of the process of learning, and develop the means for large groups of people to acquire this learning quickly and easily.

In ten years of working with people in organizations - and students in universities - I have found that the best way to help people learn the rules of the game, quickly and easily, is to talk about "pyramids and circles." Several assumptions about people and organization underlie this view of the rules: (1) it is important to recognize that, by and large, when anything important is accomplished, people are working *together*, or, in other words, nobody does anything significant on his or her own; (2) and that when people work together effectively over time, they develop certain patterns of behavior which are relatively predictable and understandable to all of those involved; (3) and further that these patterns of behavior consistently approximate certain forms, either the hierarchical pyramid or the flat circle; and (4) finally, in each of these forms, the pyramid and the circle, people interact with each other, consistently and over time, according to certain sets of rules. The rules associated with the pyramid and the circle, observable among many different sorts of people in many, many settings, are those which commonly, *without our knowing it*, shape much of our thought and behavior.

From the late 1940s through the early 1970s, pyramids - the pyramidal form - established the unspoken rules for corporate, for-profit organizations, while circles - the circular form - established the rules for educational, governmental, not-for-profit organizations. The rules of the pyramid or the rules of the circle were learned slowly over time by employees within these institutions and, often, the rules served them well over a lifetime. They did not know that they were rules but rather "just the way things were." Those who followed the rules in either the private or the public sector and who followed them well, won the game.

Since the middle 1970s, however, environmental upheavals have required that organizations become more flexible and that institutions in both the private and public sectors of the economy learn the rules of both pyramids and circles and have the adaptability to play by the set of rules most appropriate for the moment. This means that the people in organizations *must know more than one set of rules and know how to apply these rules to different situations.* In short, players on today's organizational gameboards must *know the rules and know how to learn the rules.* They must, in fact, recognize the forms of pyramids and circles, be able to play by the rules associated with each form, and switch from one form to the other according to the needs of a changing organization in a turbulent environment.

The power of the unspoken rules in affecting our behavior is often most visible when the rules have been *misunderstood* and we are faced with the resentment, anger or inertia (passive resistance) which prevents the accomplishment of our goals - and dreams. When we think that we do things alone, or when we pretend we are doing one thing when we really do another, we are demonstrating a lack of understanding of the basic patterns in which people relate to each other. The results of such misunderstanding diminish our organizational productivity and our individual satisfaction. Our lack of understanding may, in fact, shut down any of the gameboards we have come to take for granted and bring us to a precipitous and unwelcome end of the game.

The very survival of the world as we know it, therefore, depends on our gaining conscious control over the rules which shape our lives so that we develop the ability to move between changing sets of rules in a changing and unpredictable environment. Understanding pyramids and circles, then, and the rules of behavior in each form, is a prerequisite for our own welfare, that of our organizations, and of our society as a whole.

Much of the content of this book first appeared in the

1984 publication of **Flexible Organization**[1] and has as much relevance today as it did just a few years ago. In the Preface to that book I wrote:

> In the past several years, American corporations have been forced by economic circumstances to examine their foundations and to build new structures to guide a process of organizational change. The desired outcome is increased organizational effectiveness. The process of change has been one of both despair and hope, of individual deprivation and individual opportunity, of organizational failure and organizational success. The result may well be a reshaping of the American industrial complex, with widespread ramifications for all other areas of our society.
>
> This book is the product of my own involvement in the process of organizational change. I have worked with colleagues for several years to develop a new approach to studying people in organizations. Much of the theory and research that support this work is presented in the book **Organizational Sync,**[2] a forerunner of this one. As we have developed theory and conducted research, however, we also have been involved with the *process* of change in major corporations. In our work with management and supervisory units at Michigan Bell Telephone, National Broadcasting Corporation, Ford Motor Company, and General Motors Company, we have helped groups of managers conceptualize their own change process, establish goals, and implement plans to guide that process. We have learned as much from them as they have from us - maybe more - and this book is largely a result of those experiences.

In the years since its publication, I have found myself going back again and again to the message in **Flexible Organization;** it is a message which has immediate application

[1] Forisha-Kovach, B. **Flexible Organization.** Englewood Cliffs, New Jersey: Prentice-Hall, 1984

[2] Forisha-Kovach, B. **Organizational Sync.** Englewood Cliffs, NJ: Prentice-Hall, 1983.

to the lives of even more people today than four years ago. By casting the message in a new form - in the guise of the organizational gameboard - I hope to make the message clearer and more immediate to the reader. It is a message that we need to heed if we are going to be satisfied and productive members of organizations in the "continuous white waters of our time."

In the previous book I acknowledged the contributions of the many who worked with me: the initial formulation of the ideas in work with Nancy Badore and other executives at Ford Motor Company; the clarification of these ideas in extensive work with managers at Rochester Products, Division of General Motors; the tireless patience of many students at the University of Michigan - Dearborn who had a hand in completing the research that underlies the message of the book; and, particularly, my associates in Human Systems Analysis, Glenn Morris and Patricia Kosinar, and especially my husband, partner and co-founder, Randy Kovach, with all of whom I shared the delights and difficulties of creating, over time, a working team.

Today, there are many others whose ideas, support and encouragement have made this second book possible. Positive responses to the initial book by John Heldrich, Vice-President of Administration for Johnson and Johnson, Richard (Skip) LeFauve, President of Saturn Corporation of General Motors, Flora Mancuso Edwards, President of Middlesex County College, Sara Jane Koperski, Manager of Business Planning at AT&T, and Donald Peterson, Dean of the Graduate School of Applied and Professional Psychology, were instrumental in validating the importance of the message and its applicability to our current organizational situation. Intensive discussions on related questions with these individuals and many others confirm the direction taken by this book - suggesting only that given the crisis nature of our times it may not, in fact, go far enough in a needed direction.

All of those named above have now joined me in the venture of establishing the Leadership Development Institute in the School of Business at Rutgers University. Yet, just prior to undertaking this commitment this summer, I was Dean of University College on the same campus for the previous four years. The support of my senior staff at University College was critically important in the preparation of this manuscript. Without their continued willingness to work, to change, and to maintain a sense of humor, little would have been accomplished in these years. Special appreciation is due to my former colleagues at University College: Associate Dean Norbert (Gabby) Hartman, Assistant Deans John Rutan, Ed Regan, Elena Buchanan and Vicki Brooks, and Administrative Assistant Carolyn Broadbelt as well as Administrative Assistant Joan Riese who is now essential to the welfare of the Leadership Development Institute.

Yet, this book as other manuscripts would never see the light of day without the conscientious and sometimes painful editing of my research assistant, Sharon Greenfield, whose green pen has marked up every page - with an uncompromising commitment to an almost unapproachable ideal of clarity and precision in the written word.

As always, however, those who are most part of the book and the core of my support system are my family: my mother who actually *liked* this particular book, my eldest daughter who is willing to type conscientiously and edit sporadically, and most importantly, my husband Randy, who has undertaken the difficult task of supervising all of our joint ventures, at home and at work, and who has the remarkable quality of seeing each one through no matter what the difficulties.

One of the key messages of the book is that we only survive and prosper by working with others - we never do it alone. For the opportunity to talk and work with many, many others, each of whom has contributed to this product, I am grateful.

Barbara E. Kovach
New Brunswick, New Jersey
September, 1988

INTRODUCTION

What does it take to make an organization survive through difficult times? This is a question that has gained a new urgency in today's unstable, turbulent economic environment. Big corporations are in trouble. Lifetime employees in these organizations are experiencing totally unanticipated tremors of uncertainty about their own future and that of their corporations. The survivors on the big corporate scene are finding ways to emulate smaller businesses by doing things in small units and by advocating internal entrepreneurship. At the same time the percentage of people in small businesses is growing - either by choice or necessity - and many more individuals are struggling against odds which say that only a few small businesses will survive their initial decade. Thus, both in and out of our big corporations, many more individuals now need to know how to make things work and how to make an organization effective. What worked yesterday does not work today. In companies across the country, individuals are now exploring new methods to achieve organizational success.

Power and Community

What actually works is something we have known all along but have never implemented very well, namely, that organizations which function effectively are operating in two major life dimensions - each of which serves a valid function and plays an important role. What works is to acknowledge that both the *needs of the task* and the *needs of the people* must be taken into account. What works is for individuals to be both evaluating and accepting, achieving and compassionate, able to give directions and open to suggestions at the same time. What works is for us to learn to move easily between two dimensions, one of power and one of community, and thus to double the options we have available in response to any given situation.

Most of us know this to be true; we have known for a long time. However, most of us do not do this very well. If we must get something done, we live exclusively in the power dimension: we evaluate others, we give directions, and we do not listen to nor recognize others as whole human beings. On the other hand, if we believe in working *with* others and generating new ideas, we live exclusively in the community dimension: we chat and brainstorm but we hesitate to evaluate others, to urge them toward a goal, or to hold them to deadlines.

The obvious but elusive point is that if our organizations are to survive, if we are to survive as a free people, we must give up this one-dimensional way of thinking. We must learn to listen *and* evaluate, appreciate others as people *and* meet deadlines, give directions *and* welcome input from others. We must be able to do *both* things in the *same* setting with the *same* people. We must learn to function in two dimensions not just one.

The Necessity of Change

Until recently, we did not need to understand how to run

organizations well. Supported by superior resources and captive markets whatever we did worked; we had the time and the resources to wait out false starts, quality problems, and labor dissatisfactions. Having control of the marketplace provided a comfortable cushion for those in organizations. Learning, thinking, re-evaluating old ways of being was not necessary. What worked yesterday worked today - at least through the mid-1970s.

Since that time, however, increasingly stiff competition from abroad has challenged American supremacy in both resources and markets and has made the need for change imperative. As Americans we can no longer afford to dally; we have to learn to do it right the first time. In order to do this we have to reach a new level of understanding about organizations. Many organizational experts tell us that effective organizations are flexible organizations, that is, those that are able to match appropriate organizational responses to environmental realities - quickly and well. What makes organizations effective is to have the greatest possible repertoire of behaviors from which to choose, and to be able to select the right behavior for any given situation.

In short, effective organizations today, and those promising to be effective tomorrow, are those capable of changing in response to a shifting social and economic environment. A flexible resiliency is required not unyielding strength. The old analogy of the oak blowing over and breaking in the wind while the bamboo reed bends and stands up straight again is applicable to our situation. What was certain yesterday is uncertain today. What were accepted practices before are missing the mark in our current situation. Such a situation demands that organizations view changing circumstances as opportunities for refining goals, reevaluating objectives, and increasing productivity in directions that meet the needs of a new reality. Organizations must change despite the slow and painful process of change - and changing, emerge stronger.

Balance and Flexibility

The keys to individual and organizational success are balance and flexibility. In ourselves, in groups and organizations, we must balance getting things done *and* concern for others, giving directions *and* eliciting others' opinions, being independent *and* being a team member. In short, we must balance the dimensions of power and community in order to promote flexibility, so that in any given situation we have a choice between at least two, and possible more, alternatives. Such flexibility is critical to our survival. What we do now matters.

This book is about how to achieve this balance and this flexibility in ourselves and in our workplaces. In order to do this we need first to to think about differences - among people and within organizations. We have to acknowledge the different strengths of the many players; we have to understand the different rules that are in force at different times, in different areas, of our organizations. Then, armed with an understanding of differences, we can work toward achieving a balance of many different strengths, and from these different strengths build strong organizations.

We have no time to waste. If we continue to believe that almost everybody is alike and that there is but one way to do things, America will continue its slow downhill slide. If we recognize instead the diversity of talent in our workplaces, and become strong in both power (getting things done) and community (sharing with others), we will increase the strength and resiliency of our organizations. If we shrug off this responsibility to become agents of change, movers and shakers in our systems, our children will not have the choices that we have enjoyed in our lifetime. If we do not bring about a greater awareness of differences as the foundation for renewed organizational flexibility, America as a whole will not have the ability to respond effectively to the dramatic changes which mark our times. The choice is ours . . .

The Organizational Gameboard

The image of a gameboard on which small pieces representing human figures move along predefined paths according to specific rules is one which bears many similarities to our lives in organizations. The rules in organizations establish the limits for appropriate behavior at any particular place and time. Variations of the rules may be applicable as well, depending on the location, the task, and the dimension (either power or community) predominating at a given moment in time. Through most of American corporate history, these rules have been fairly predictable, variations expected and understandable, and complete deviations episodic and short-lived.

Today, unexpected occurrences are more frequent - so frequent, in fact, that the unexpected is assuming a certain regularity. Yet the rules guiding human behavior have not changed; rather the rapidity with which one must shift *between* sets of rules has increased dramatically. In fact the changes of the last decade *require* that all individuals must learn to move between the two dimensions of power and community, in order to bring to their organizations the balance and flexibility essential for survival.

As the environment becomes increasingly unpredictable, it becomes even more important to recognize the rules governing behavior in groups, especially in organizations. We must know how to sense a new variation in the rules, how to recognize new expectations, and then how to make our individual decisions based on this knowledge. For too many people sudden shifts in the environment lead only to discomfort and fear: discomfort because what was known is no longer valid, and fear because any remaining familiarity might be swept away. For these people, the legacy of a previously regular but now seemingly chaotic organizational experience is frustration and bitterness. If instead they were to understand that the old rules of power and community still govern human affairs and that we need only to increase our sensitivity to and expertise in each dimension, they might be able to find an inner anchor in such understanding and to look upon the unexpected as a challenge.

However, we need not only to be sensitive to the rules of the organizational game in times of rapid shifts, but also sensitive to similarities and differences among ourselves, the players in this game. Similarities form the basis for the dimension of community: we are all very much like one another, and therefore can accept and respect one another, sharing our ideas and experiences. Differences among us form the basis for the dimension of power: we bring different skills, abilities and perspectives to our organizations and thus can do much more working together than any one of us can alone.

Once we know the rules and the players at any given point in time, we are well equipped to play the game and to make the most of opportunities emerging from change. Anchored in such understanding, the legacy of our organizational experience is likely to be a sense of meaning, relatedness and accomplishment - and awareness of making a positive contribution to the welfare of those who walked with us and those who come behind. What we do matters not only for ourselves and our immediate companions but for all who follow. The future of our organizations depends on how well we know the rules and the players, and on how well we play the game.

On Reading this Book

What this book is about can be gleaned primarily from the straightforward descriptions of people and organizations which form the body of each chapter. The message is illustrated with stories about people working in organizations, as well as with graphic charts and diagrams. The important points can be grasped quickly by reading the body of each chapter, examining the charts and diagrams, and skimming over the examples. For most readers this material can be covered in an evening or two.

The material is briefly introduced with a gameboard analogy, which appears in italics at the beginning of each chapter. For some readers, this may offer another perspective on the message of the book. Others, who have less enthusiasm for story-telling, would do well to skip these sections and go right to the central part of each chapter.

Each chapter is followed by an exercise designed to give you another way to look at yourself, others, or your organization. Again, for some people such exercises are more useful than for others. For those who profit from working through this material, more related exercises can be found in the last appendix of the book, along with solutions for the exercises and commentaries where appropriate.

Read this book in the way which suits you best, either quickly or slowly, in part or totally. It is my hope that this perspective on organizations will increase understanding, thus adding to the zest with which each of us plays the organizational game. For almost all of us, working in organizations is the only game in town and how we play it now matters not only to ourselves but to those who follow after us.

TABLE OF CONTENTS

TABLE OF FIGURES

TABLE OF EXERCISES

The
Organizational
Gameboard

Winning the
Game at Work
in Changing Times

One:
The Organizational Gameboard

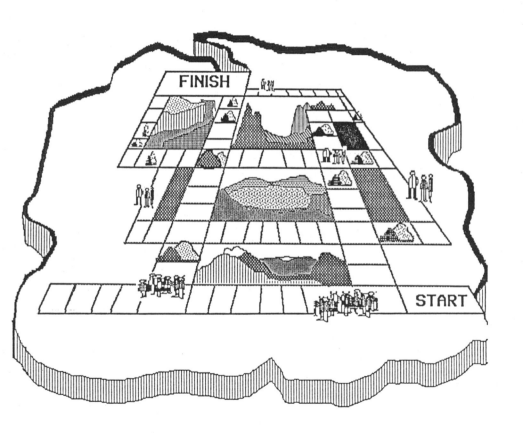

Most of us play out our lives on organizational gameboards. As we enter the organizational game at "start," we think that we know the rules and that we will win the game - exiting at "finish" with self-respect, influence, recognition and material rewards. Most often, however, we give up our dreams along the way, content to exit long before the finish box, with a more modest set of rewards. Our expectations change as we play the game; we trade in more distant adventures for the comfort of familiar surroundings. We, the players, give up our dreams in order to stay with others like ourselves in a known locale, finding in group identity a sustaining sense of belonging.

So it has been. However, the winds of change are sweeping across the gameboards, shifting the terrain, rearranging the players, and upsetting the rules. There is little comfort to be found in following familiar routines, for the tasks and the setting have shifted considerably. There is little hope of retreating into a familiar group, for many of the players have been scattered to other spaces on the gameboard, bounced onto other organizational boards, or left these boards to play out the game on boards circumscribed by the family and community. Thus the rules and the players have been quickly and repeatedly changing, and there seems to be no profit in doing today what was done yesterday.

Where, then, can individuals find the satisfaction and sense of belonging that had previously brought meaning to their lives? Only in accepting the changes, learning from them, and growing in understanding of the rules and the players. Through a greater understanding and action based on this understanding, can the players today find any sense of security in an uncertain world.

Outlining the Game

Our organizational gameboard is large and of irregular shape. Lines of little squares criss-cross the board in every possible direction, moving across uneven terrain with both hills and valleys. The squares are sometimes wide enough for many to travel together, sometimes narrow and barely visible through the underbrush. Looking toward the distant horizon, we might glimpse a patchwork of other such gameboards dotting the landscape, each board of irregular size and shape, with hills and valleys, and with wide and narrow roads and pathways.

Strong gusts of wind blow across the boards from time to time, rearranging the location of hills and valleys on a given board and shifting the lines of squares to new places. What was here yesterday is not the same today: valleys exist where there were once only hills, new hills arise in what were once valleys. The maps of yesterday no longer relate to the paths on the gameboard. The game itself is new.

The Players

Across each board we see many small figures like ourselves moving along from square to square, each one playing the game. Many of these players appear to stay on only one gameboard all their working lives, moving one square at a time along only one of the lines. Others hop from board to board, leaving and entering in the middle of various games. Still others never really get into the game: they begin at start, wobble a little and then fall down along the edge, repeating this on one board or another innumerable times.

The players are not evenly spaced along the boards. Near the starting box, many travel together on wide roads. Near the finish of each game, a smaller number travel in little groups helping each other up and down rocky cliff faces and walking single file on narrow trails. There are many at the beginning of each game and few at the end for all through the game players exit at a variety of mid-points, having been stuck in either the hills or valleys and never finishing the course.

The Rules

*The players on the hills and valleys each know the rules of accepted behavior for their particular location. Those in the hills (focused on achievement) believe they have the **only** rules and tell each other of the anarchy which reigns in the valleys. Those in the valleys (focused on sharing and communication) believe that they have the **only** rules and tell each other of the loneliness which characterizes those in the hills. Only the travelers who cross both the hills and valleys recognize that there are at least two viable sets of rules and that individuals may live by **both** sets of rules depending which is appropriate at the time.*

The End of the Game

The travelers on the gameboard are few in number. Working well in the hills and valleys and acquiring an overview of the entire board, they are yet outnumbered many times by those who work only in the hills and valleys. It is the collective weight of the many players that keeps the gameboard in position and keeps the game alive for another round.

Many of the players are threatened by the winds of change - and with good reason. Each time the winds blow across the hills and through the valleys, they sweep a significant number of players off the board and out of the game. Yet, it is more often the travelers who survive - not bound to a certain place or a certain way of working, they are more likely to move with the winds instead of being buffeted by them.

But all players suffer from each loss. As the total number of players diminishes, the game itself is less likely to continue. With decreasing numbers of players, it is likely that any particular gameboard will be taken over by those on another board. Then, for the original players, the game is over and these players may never return to an organizational gameboard again.

If our organizations are going to survive as productive entities, they must develop many more people who are able to live well in two dimensions - and not just in one. Like those on the gameboard, the number of travelers (living in two dimensions) is in short supply, and the numbers stuck on hills and in valleys (living a one-dimensional existence) is large.

People in organizations must acknowledge the benefits - in fact the absolute necessity - of developing the dimensions of both power and community. In so doing, they achieve the balance that is the basis of individual flexibility. Then, organizations themselves, composed of many such individuals, will also become flexible and responsive to their environment. The old ways now provide no guarantees though we may tell ourselves that they do, for both the players and the rules have changed.

Changing Players, Changing Rules

When people enter organizations they often become attached to others who have entered the organization at about the same time. These individuals then become an informal group. Members of such groups often act as a team, helping each other to overcome obstacles and to circumvent roadblocks. Many of their expectations about their progress are strongly tied to their unconscious assumptions about their relationships with their informal team. Knowing that one is working with the same people provides a measure of security to individuals in organizations. Yet as the forces of change sweep across the organizational landscape, all of us must adjust to the changes that occur in our significant groups and our major connections with others.

There are many examples of people who experience a negative impact on their careers when players change. One division manager of a major company attributed a recent career slowdown to a corporate reshuffling of the players resulting in his finding himself without a "sponsor," someone of higher status than he to look out for his welfare. Managers at a General Motors manufacturing facility who lost their sponsors and protectors in an organizational turnaround quit to seek out other opportunities. Other groups of managers temporarily suffered lower productivity in their departments when corporate moves upset important work relationships. Thus, the sense of belonging to a team and of having predictable and positive relationships is central to the way in which people evaluate their careers and future possibilities. Yet this can no longer provide the security it once did.

Yet not only have the players changed but the rules have changed as well. Individuals playing the game for a while need to become aware that the rules in effect when they began have changed during the course of the game. Those who continue to be most productive - helping themselves and others to finish the course - are those who have learned to play by new sets of rules. They recognize that an occasional toss of the dice introduces a chance factor into their progress

- times when all the rules may be off for a moment - but realize that, by and large, progress along the gameboard comes from playing by the rules - whether they are the ones under which they entered or the new ones introduced along the way.

Examples of needing to learn new rules exist on many fronts. Corporate managers have had to "think differently" about their jobs because of the new factors introduced by the economic turbulence of the 1980s. Managers in the auto companies, in particular, have had to carve out a whole new set of rules in order to operate in a competitive environment in which they no longer have the top hand. Managers at AT&T are struggling with the same issues as the telephone company's divestiture has put Ma Bell into a competitive scramble with other communications companies, removing the security of a lock on the market which had sheltered this company for decades.

The resentment and anger of employees asked to adopt a new set of game rules can halt a company's progress and stop the game. On the other hand, employees' willingness to venture into new territory can set leadership patterns that improve the product and the service of any company more than ever before. The ways in which employees respond to changing rules is a clear indicator of the future welfare of any organization.

Managing the Change Process

The fact is that given the current economic turbulence (which is not expected to lessen in the foreseeable future), we will all be working in organizations where rules and players change on a fairly regular basis. Circumstances require that we develop the flexibility to adapt to these changes. We need to take greater advantage of the opportunities for growth inherent in all changing situations and focus less on the losses which also accompany change. Changes in rules and working relationships require that we all change and that we reevaluate many of the assumptions that have supported us in the past.

When changes occur within an organization, people are forced to take a new look at reality. This means seriously looking at how things are and not pretending that things are the way we might like them to be. When we are open to finding out what is going on inside and around us we become privy to a tremendous amount of information - about ourselves, others and the organization - which we might have shut out in the past.

As we monitor ourselves and others, as we question our own assumptions and withhold evaluations of other people, we learn more about how systems work. The farther out beyond ourselves we can reach in terms of broadening our information base the more solid will be the knowledge on which we later act. If we go beyond ourselves and even beyond the organization, paying attention to the social and economic changes which are occurring outside, we will walk more surely along the narrow road between naivete and cynicism. In this way, we will be preparing ourselves for the leadership roles necessary for the survival both of our individual selves and of our organizational worlds.

Two:
The Process of Organizational Change

*In times gone past players on the gameboards believed that they were responsive to change, in fact, that they sought it out. "How did the gameboards come about in the first place?" they asked each other rhetorically. "Because we wanted to find the best way to do something, no matter what the cost," came the expected answer. These players have been telling themselves this for years. Yet, the players who **did** explore new territiries, who **did** build, design and create the gameboards, started playing the game a long, long time ago. Since then change has come to be viewed more as an enemy than as a friend.*

Given the pioneering spirit of yesterday's players, some of the players today are puzzled to find themselves fearful of the changes wrought by the gusting winds. Those stuck on the hills and in the valleys have had little experience with the process of change, and do not connect the changes of today with those which their own ancestors managed and created in times gone past. They only hope (against all reason) that the winds will pass by their own valley or hill, leaving them as they were.

Americans have historically been a people who believe in change and in adventure. In fact, change has often been viewed as meaningful merely for its own sake; that is, people would choose to do something new because it was new, whether or not it was better. However, as our country has grown from adolescence to maturity, its people have developed a stronger attachment to stability and the *status quo*. More recently, we seem to like things the way they are

- or the way they were - and are reluctant to face the prospect of a living and working according to a new set of rules. Furthermore, once we find ourselves forced to change we want to do so instantly, and to get the transition over with all at once. Just emerging from our societal adolescence, we still tend to dream about instant transformations in which the old gives way to the new overnight. It is more difficult to accept the fact that genuine change in both people and institutions is slow, complex, and incremental (see Figure 2.1)

Figure 2.1

THE NATURE OF CHANGE

1. SLOW

Events which instigate change may be abrupt but genuine.

Change which integrates new patterns of expectations and behavior occurs only over time.

2. COMPLEX

Change in any part of a system affects all other parts.

3. INCREMENTAL

New behaviors are learned and integrated one step at a time with much trial and error along the way.

Change is Slow

People accept change slowly. Although it may appear that the rules and players of any game we play change overnight, it takes a long time for people to adapt to a new setting. Although specific events that instigate change in human affairs may at times appear sudden, shocking, and abrupt, the actual changes in human behavior occur only over time. Mt. St. Helens did erupt overnight; the merger of Stroh's and Schaefer's was finalized in one day; the deregulation of AT&T became a fact at the start of 1983. But even apparently sudden changes are often years in the making. Most often it takes much longer than one day or one night for human beings to absorb these kinds of changes, and to create patterns that respond appropriately to them. Permanent change, in people and in systems, takes place only over time. The process of transforming the old into the new occurs by fits and starts, and is not complete until individuals and systems have integrated and stabilized new patterns of behavior. The effects of such change - and the benefits - may become apparent only after a year or more has passed.

For example, the official act of signing a merger may precede by years the former employees of one company trusting and respecting the former employees of the other company. The deregulation of major utility companies may not for quite awhile affect the practices of many managers reared in the good old days, when the style of management was different. Only slowly may such managers opt for change or early retirement, in the meantime influencing company practices for years. Changes in human systems usually trail behind changes in official organizational documents and executive policy. Individuals change slowly, and systems composed of many individuals change even more slowly.

When Bob Thomasen, a supervisor in an engineering division of a manufacturing company, attended a training program, he developed some new patterns of behavior. As he began to apply this behavior in the workplace, his employees became suspicious of the motives for this change. Bob had always been an authoritarian so-and-so, bossing his people around. Now he was asking them for their opinions (even though he always gave them a five-minute lecture after they responded) and occasionally he told a joke and stood around with his men on the floor. His employees wondered what was going on. They wondered if he was setting them up - and consequently set him up by coming in late and not putting equipment away. When he responded in his old dictatorial way, they smiled and said, "see, he hasn't changed at all." But Bob **had** changed, and after this outburst he redoubled his efforts to develop a style that involved his employees more often. One year later, Bob and his employees have developed a new level of trust for one another - and the department is much more participative than formerly. Change occurred - but only over time did new patterns of behavior become a stable part of the human system.

Change is Complex

We all live in overlapping systems where individuals are interdependent with many others. Change in one part of a system affects all the other parts. Most of us, for example, are part of organizational systems where we work in one unit, and are also members of committees or task forces with members from many units. All are systems in themselves.

Then we may also live in families, and have circles of friends and community associations. Tension generated by changing the leadership on one committee may affect our performance on a task force as well as our work in general. We may bring this tension home, where our family members may spread it to the rest of their own associations as well as to ours.

When Bob Thomasen began to change his behavior at work, the changes affected not only his immediate employees but his family as well. Just as he had always told his workers what to do, he also had always told his wife and children what to do. His family, just as his employees, had been used to the old obnoxious behavior. Suddenly they were puzzled, confused, and uncertain. His children wondered if something was the matter with Dad. Ultimately they too had to learn some new behaviors.

Additionally, the change that was occurring in Bob's work unit impinged on another work unit. As Bob Thomasen's employees got themselves together with his new style of behavior, their unit became more effective. A second unit watching from the sidelines, had always been the leader in productivity and had regarded itself as a model of organizational effectiveness. As the men in this group watched Bob's unit become more productive, they became disgruntled and began telling Bob's employees that this was all a con job on Bob's part and that they should not listen. Their challenges to Bob's employees were passed on to Bob. Only when Bob persisted in his new ways, and persuaded his employees to do the same, did the second unit begin to accept that something new was happening. Slowly, some new ideas spread into the second unit, and after a year or so, the changes that Bob had begun were finally accepted practices.

Bob's unit was closely connected with only one other unit. If it had interfaced with a number of other units, changes in Bob's department would have been even *more* difficult, because each of those departments would have had to change in response to Bob's. Each of them would have had to create some new rules and possibly, eventually, rearrange their players. Thus, the larger the complex of overlapping systems the more slowly does change occur. In each new area the changes must overcome members' resistance as more and more groups respond to changed behaviors in other units.

Organizational change is effective only when individual behavior actually changes. On the other hand, changes in key individuals' behavior causes eventual change in the system. In each organizational area, established ways of doing things have been written down in policy booklets, with the weight of the past often measurable by the amount of organizational paper that has accumulated on the subject. Change throughout a system, therefore, often means discarding or rewriting the rulebooks of the past that legitimize those behavior patterns. Changes in behavior eventually mean changes in the rules. And changes in the rules sometimes force changes in the player. Change affects not just one part of an organizational system, but *all* of it.

Change is Incremental

Change happens one bit at a time. People do not accept new behavioral patterns overnight. The implementation of new behavior between divisions of a major corporation may begin with something as small as enforcing the letter of the law in one small section of order forms used to send information back and forth between divisions. If this new practice is established, and over time increases the effectiveness of the two units' interaction, other ways to increase effectiveness may also be agreed upon. The first steps in change often seem small and insignificant but are the stepping stones for later activities of larger scope. The acceptance of Quality Circles - a new way of problem-solving for workers - in a manufacturing setting begins with the success of just one circle; when others see the results, they want to be successful too. Within a year or two, there may be a great many successful Quality Circles in that setting.

Just like learning to walk, change proceeds one step at a time. Toddlers fall down a lot because they have not yet quite gotten the hang of this new behavior. Just so, as individuals and systems experiment with new behaviors they are bound to make mistakes, to be clumsy in implementation, and to do things poorly. Effective behavior requires practice and is perfected only slowly. When Bob Thomasen finally learned to smile, he said he felt as if his smile were cracking his face. In fact, it looked rather like it was, but he got better over time. Effectiveness comes with practice. Consequently, in systems change there are many ups and downs as new behaviors, procedures and policies are implemented, reevaluated and often redesigned until they are flowing in harmony with each other.

Change is Paradoxical

At each step along the path of change there are both opportunities and limitations. Not only is change slow, complex, and incremental but it is also paradoxical. The forces of change eradicate old ways of being at the same time as they create opportunities for new and more constructive ones. The loss of old ways of being is almost always experienced as painful although there may be excitement in the possibilities that open up. Individuals caught in the throes of change thus experience their worlds as both contracting and expanding at once. They are required to adjust to the necessities of retrenchment and the imperatives for innovation at the same time. They must learn to play by new rules of a new game (see Figure 2.2).

Figure 2.2

THE PARADOXICAL NATURE OF CHANGE

Shrinkage	VS	Expansion
Retrenchment	VS	Innovation
Loss	VS	Opportunity
Adaptation	VS	Leadership

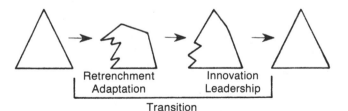

Retrenchment Innovation
Adaptation Leadership
Transition

An administrative official at the University of Michigan commented in the midst of the recession of the early 1980s that university administrators seemed to be living a schizophrenic existence. On the one hand, they would spend four hours in a meeting deciding which units and sometimes which faculty were going to be cut back in order to meet new budget requirements; and, on the other hand, they would go to another long meeting to explore new possibilities for university facilities and faculty to contribute to the corporate community. They would cut back old programs and start up new ones which promised greater productivity down the road. The juxtaposition of the cutbacks and the expansion was sometimes enough to make a person's head spin. It was often difficult to live with both at the same time.

However, it is possible to take advantage of the opportunities afforded by changing circumstances only if individuals are willing to live with both retrenchment and innovation simultaneously. The demands of retrenchment cannot be ignored, and we must turn our attention to them. However, whether we choose to make use of the opportunities as well is up to us. If we fail to do so, then we will know only the pain of change - the sense of giving up something important - and not the possibilities for growth. Our world will contract and our possibilities narrow.

However, if we meet the demands for letting go of what has been at the same time that we create what will be, we can shape the course of change. Retrenching under pressure is adaptation. Creating a new course is leadership. In times of instability and uncertainty, the leaders who emerge will adapt to overwhelming forces and shape new directions - both at the same time. They are the ones who will move up and play the game successfully on a changing gameboard.

Focus on Process

These leaders will understand that change is a process and not a product, that living in transition requires that individuals focus on how things are done as well as what is to be accomplished. Thus, for a while, the rewards for individuals and organizations will come from handling the process well and from creating organizations that respond to the challenges of change. Succeeding means, in fact, living in the meantime, for individuals in uncertain times experience themselves as neither here nor there, but rather as in between.

How business is transacted in the coming years will be of paramount importance for each individual and each organization. The rules of the game are changing, and as they change so do the players. People are moving up and down; many leave companies, some create their own. The familiarity of a stable system can no longer provide individuals with a sense of security and comfort.

Playing the game well and accomplishing things that matter have always been great sources of satisfaction in the organizational world. Today, understanding what's happening - in the organization and in oneself - is the greatest source of security available on a changing board. We must learn the new rules, and we must learn how to work well on changing teams with different players. The satisfactions derived from such efforts will be stronger, deeper, and more often marked by joy than any satisfactions gained from clinging to old rules and believing that things won't change - today or tomorrow.

The foundation for success on this changing board is understanding. Understanding of self, other people, and the organization are the building blocks of leadership, the tools with which to take an active hand in the process of organizational change. The leaders of tomorrow will be drawn from those who have this understanding.

As you read this book you might ask yourself the following questions. How do I respond to change? How do I create effective organizations? What new directions do I choose? What old directions do I give up? For you, and for any given individual in an organization, the answers to these questions are determined by the strengths that emerge from the process of knowing onself and the possibilities that become visible through the process of growing to understand one's organizations. Those who grow in understanding will find an excitement on the new gameboard not present in previous times. Those who act on this understanding will be the leaders who contribute to the survival and enhancement of America as a world power.

Each of the following chapters is designed to provide a framework for understanding organizational functioning and individual strengths and the interplay between them that takes us farther down the road to organizational flexibility and effectiveness.

EXERCISE: PROBLEMS AND OPPORTUNITIES IN CHANGE

1. List some of the problems that you see arising in your organization because of recent changes in the economic environment.

2. If possible, discuss with others in your organization the items that you have listed. Can you agree on three items that present the greatest problems or carry the greatest risks for your organization?

3. For each of the items you listed state at least one way in which each problem presents new opportunities for the organization.

Three:
The Rules of the Game
in Pyramids and Circles

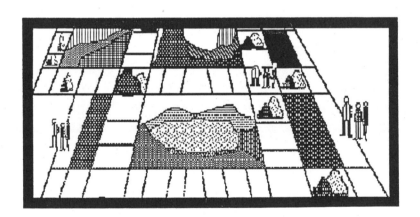

The winds of change gust across the boards at erratic times in unpredictable patterns - in the eyes of the players. The travelers are the only ones who are not terrified by the possibilities inherent in those winds. When the winds begin to whistle, the players in the valleys cling to each other and those on the hills stand even straighter and taller and feel more alone, each praying that in being even more like they are, they will withstand the forces of change. Yet they remain unprepared, and when the wind changes their valley into a hill or their hill into a valley, they are often blown away by the gusts, to try their hand at a new organizational gameboard or to leave the organizational game altogether.

In contrast, gameboard travelers perceive the winds as adding new challenges and opportunities to their journey as they continue onward toward the finish of the game. Each band of travelers is a working team, blazing trails for others to follow, recognizing that their collective strength emerged from their very differences - and that none would make it to the end alone.

Those working in American organizations must learn to live in the dimensions of both power and community: they must get things done and at the same time work in harmony with others, sharing experiences and ideas, and thinking beyond the present. All of us at work must increase our repertoire of behaviors and then match the appropriate behavior to the appropriate situation. The first is important because organizations require a wide variety of available responses to adapt to unpredictable demands on a changing gameboard. The second is critical because matching the right response to a given situation - making the right move in the game - determines the success or failure of the organization.

Balance is the Name of the Game

Organizations increase their range of alternative behaviors and possibilities by developing strength in two dimensions. They strengthen the dimension associated with community by encouraging all their employees to generate ideas and possible solutions to current situations. They increase strength in the power dimension by developing systems and procedures with which to implement action once an alternative is selected. Organizations need a full repertoire of behaviors in order for organizational members to be able to think, to plan, and to act from the widest possible base of information.

Most organizations do not have a history of meeting each of these needs equally well. Rather they tend to fall into one of two camps - emphasizing either the importance of generating ideas, or the importance of acting - rather than a combination of the two. Many industrial giants, for example, have failed to encourage their employees to generate ideas to solve current problems. On the other hand, many governmental, educational, and social service institutions have not developed the implementation systems to act on ideas with appropriate speed. In both cases, organizations fail to respond with maximum flexibility to current environmental exigencies.

Choosing the Right Move

In order to produce the most successful outcome, organizations must (1) have a thorough knowledge of a given situation and the possible consequences of alternative actions, and (2) have individuals in decision-making capacities who can filter and evaluate this information utilizing the broadest possible frame of reference. They need to know as much as possible about the situation, including both human and technological factors, and they must be able to evaluate what they know from a systems-wide perspective, which includes an awareness of the past as well as possibilities for the future.

Effective decisions are based on information. In times of change, organizations need to know what is happening in the wider world, what is occurring within their own system, and how the people in that system might react to various courses of action. This means that they need excellent communication systems. First, they require as many individuals as possible to act as sources of information, reporting on both external and internal events. Therefore, they need to encourage individuals who have access to information to look, to listen, and to share this information with others. Second, they need to create channels of communication within the organization so that all available information flows toward individuals in decision-making capacities. In many organizations this means clearing upward channels of communication, often blocked by protocol and fear.

Once the information is gathered, organizations require that individuals who can filter and evaluate this information be in decision-making positions. These individuals can take both a wide and long view. They can assess incoming information in terms of the total system, balancing potential effects on individuals against effects on the system, weighing the effects on one unit in relationship to the effects on other units. They must be able to assess this information in terms of past history and possible future consequences. They must be able to assess both short- and long-term results of immediate action and strike an effective balance between short- and long-range benefits. Finally, they must be able to act - and to accept the consequences of their action. An outcome is never guaranteed and every decision entails the risk of failure as well as possibility of success.

Different Organizational Structures

The potential for developing all of these behaviors is increased when organizations create a variety of formal and informal organizational structures. Representative of the hills on the gameboard are the pyramidal structures, tall, triangular shapes; and representative of the valleys are the circular structures, flat, round shapes. For maximum organizational flexibility and effectiveness, the pyramidal and circular structures must be in appropriate proportion to each other and suited to the task. For maximum individual productivity and satisfaction, individuals must learn how to work well within both kinds of structures, and how to tune their behavior to the unspoken rules that exist within any pyramid or circle.

Each structure has its own organizational *climate*. The climate is created by the sum of all the expectations individuals have about human behavior in a given setting. Organizational climates are, in fact, collective sets of individual expectations. And these expectations in turn strongly affect human behavior.

When individuals expect that their information, ideas and opinions will be accepted, they are more willing to contribute to the corporate pool of knowledge. When individuals expect that their ideas will be heard by those at the top, they are more willing to pass their knowledge upward. When individuals expect that their information makes a difference and affects courses of action, they become better information gatherers and selectors - and often more productive human beings.

Similarly, when individuals know what the expectations are for their work, they will turn more willingly to the task ahead. When they know that their performance will be recognized, they are more willing to put out extra effort to get the job done. Finally, when they know that their work will not only be recognized but rewarded, they are even more likely to go the extra mile to do a quality job.

In the circles and in the pyramids of every organization, the unspoken rules for behavior evolve to fit the particular structure. Individuals who cannot adjust to these different sets of rules end up stuck in either pyramidal or circular structures, in either the hills or valleys of the organizational gameboard, vulnerable to being swept off the board when struck by gusting winds of change. Recognizing the different structures and being tuned in to their different sets of rules is one of the key ingredients for success, one of the ways to insure that one stays in the game.

Yet what proportion of pyramids and circles are approriate on any organizational gameboard. We must not only function in both pyramids and circles, we must use each for an appropriate organizational purpose. If pyramids are demanded and circles supplied, or *vice versa*, our organizations will neither meet their goals nor motivate their employees. Thus we must understand not only the rules but the *functions* and *purposes* of both pyramids and circles.

Pyramids and Circles

Organizations are most effective when their members function well in both pyramids and circles, and when the proportion of pyramids and circles is appropriate for the goals, tasks and purposes of the organization (see Figure 3.1). We know the atmospheres in pyramidal and circular settings to be quite different from each other. Effective pyramids are characterized by efficiency, briskness, and a sense that things are happening. Effective circles are characterized by openness, warmth, and responsiveness to individuals. Pyramids encourage people to work hard and get things done. Circles encourage people to share their ideas with each other and to imagine new possibilities. Pyramids represent power, circles represent community. When pyramids and circles are in balance with each other, and individuals function well in both pyramids and circles, an organization is most likely to be highly effective in meeting its own goals and achieving its objectives.

Pyramids are the hierarchical systems of organizations, with a few power wielders at the top and many followers at the bottom. Pyramids symbolize power and the task dimensions of organizational activity. They are designed for getting things done. *Circles,* on the other hand, are the flat systems in organizations in which all members are relatively equal. Circles symbolize affiliation and the belief that everyone's opinion carries equal weight. They are designed for the sharing of information and ideas, providing self-confirmation for individual members.

Figure 3.1

FUNCTIONS OF PYRAMIDS AND CIRCLES

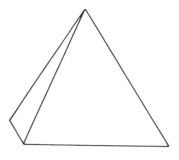

PYRAMIDS are Appropriate for
• Accomplishing Specific Tasks
• Implementing Accepted Procedures
• Doing Things Quickly

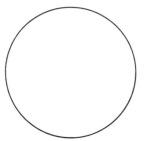

CIRCLES are Appropriate for
• Clarifying Ambiguous Situations
• Creating Lists of Alternatives
• Winning Acceptance for New Ideas

Pyramids are effective for making final decisions and for implementing action plans. Individuals at the top of pyramids who have been receptive to information from throughout the system have the capacity to see the ramifications of decisions on all units over time. From this position, they can also monitor the actions of individuals in various roles as they implement action plans. There are certain benefits to viewing situations from the top - the overall design is clearer and details are evaluated in the larger context.

Circles, in contrast, are effective for gathering information and for generating alternative courses of action. Structurally, circles lie flat against the ground and have more points of contact with their environment. They are able to absorb more information than the taller pyramid, which is more concentrated on up-and-down channels of information than on those that flow in and out. Circles are also effective for sharing ideas and generating alternatives. Individuals within circles are regarded as equals, so that individual contributions are valued and considered on their merits. The flat structure of the circle encourages the sharing of information, the formulating of possibilites, and the valuing of human beings.

The climates generated by pyramidal and circular structures are quite different. Effective pyramids are characterized by efficiency, briskness, and a sense that things are happening. Effective circles are characterized by openness, warmth, and responsiveness to individuals. Pyramids encourage people to work hard and get things done. Circles encourage people to share their ideas with each other and to imagine new possibilities.

As times are changing, many organizations are seeking to build circles where only pyramids existed before, and others are raising pyramids on what were formerly only circular structures. As individuals accustomed to living only in pyramids or circles face the need to live in both, they demonstrate resistance to learning new ways of being. Change is often painful. The rewards of going through the transition to the other side, however, are more than worth the difficulties encountered along the way.

For example, a typical pyramidal organization is exemplified by one of the automobile companies in the early 1980s. Traditionally as tall and skinny as the Eiffel Tower, it has recently been propelled by increasing losses to reevaluate its own structure. Those at the top have made the decision (in their customary autocratic manner) to flatten their organization and to develop circles at all levels of the corporation. Although circles have been introduced into the corporation and the span of control increased at all levels, old ways die hard. Managers still tell other managers what to do and these managers tell their subordinates. Subordinates keep their ideas to themselves from fear of reprisals for unwanted suggestions. Thus the process of opening up communication channels and generating new ideas among employees at all levels has begun - but the process of actually implementing these new ideas will take many years.

In contrast, a typical circular organization is often found in the public service arena, such as in one division of a public utility company - long an organization dominated by circles. The primary function of this division is to generate new ideas for marketing the company's product. In the past, the division has been very effective in the marketing area. Personnel within the division have been encouraged to be creative and innovative. In the middle 1970s, this division became part of a Quality of Work Life effort. They instituted formal circles in which employees could discuss their work and suggest solutions for problems.

The QWL philosophy fit with that of the division, and there was an easy and smooth transition from the informal to the formal circular structures. Recently, however, this division has become part of a deregulated national utility organization and has entered a competitive market. The change has shaken the division, which is now developing a new model for employee behavior. As one manager said, "We all used to wear our QWL jackets. Now, we're supposed to take them off and become 'tough managers'". Now entering a competitive arena, this company is seeking to build some pyramids amidst its circles, so that it can prosper in a competitive world.

Both of these companies learned to change the rules, and individuals within the companies learned - not always happily at first - to play by new rules. The pyramids changed by introducing circles, the circles by introducing pyramids. The "get it done" rules of the pyramid changed to include "let's take the time to sit down and talk together." The sharing, laid-back rules of the circle changed to include an emphasis on "utilizing" the best idea.

As the winds of change sweep across the organizational gameboard, they leave more opportunities for growth and expansion in their wake than they do for constriction and contraction. These opportunities however, can only be seen by those who are willing to scan the new landscape, accept the tumultuous changes and play by new rules.

Establishing a Balance

When effective pyramids and circles exist within organizations, the organizations themselves are effective. Members of the organization have the capacity to gather information, generate alternatives, select courses of action, and implement action plans. They have available to them the widest range of possible behaviors. The most effective balance of pyramids and circles depends on the overall goals of the organization and its current situation, but each organization requires such a balance. The flat circular structures absorb information from the environment and generate alternative possibilities in terms of this information. Individuals within circles develop a sense of belonging to the organization and experience themselves as influencing its course. As a consequence, ultimate decisions engage the acceptance and commitment of individual members. The hierarchical, pyramidal structures within organizations then use this information, evaluate a wealth of alternatives, make final decisions and monitor implementation. Within pyramidal structures, roles are defined and responsibilities assigned. Operating, however, from a circular base, decision makers may be confident that their decisions will be generally accepted - because all will have had an opportunity to have input into those decisions.

Lack of Balance

A scarcity of either pyramids or circles within an organization hampers its effectiveness. In stable economic times, the lack may be relatively unnoticed. In unchanging circumstances, continuous communication with the external environment is less necessary, since yesterday's information will do as well as today's. Consequently, pyramids can survive without circles. Similarly, in a stable situation, innovative, difficult, and rapid decision making is less often required since yesterday's procedures may serve as guidelines for today's actions. Thus, circles can survive without pyramids. However, in turbulent times, when much is unknown and familiar patterns are no longer viable, the lack of either effective pyramids or circles may promote rigidities of behavior which cannot adapt to changing circumstances.

Such rigidities of behavior resulting from an imbalance of pyramids and circles may be symbolized by two new structures: *crooked pyramids* and *squishy circles* (See Figure 3.2). Pyramids that stand alone in a shifting landscape lack the information and employee support to respond to rapidly changing circumstances. In self-defense, such pyramids, shuddering as the ground shifts, bend over and become crooked. As they bend, they dominate their employees, repressing innovation and new ideas.

In similar fashion, circles that stand alone in times of change lack the ability to make difficult decisions and to implement them rapidly. In the face of failure, such circles

Figure 3.2

INEFFECTIVE PYRAMIDS AND CIRCLES

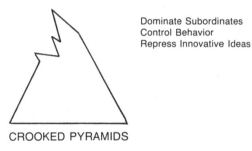

Dominate Subordinates
Control Behavior
Repress Innovative Ideas

CROOKED PYRAMIDS

Avoid Conflict
Control Behavior
Limit Information Flow

SQUISHY CIRCLES

begin to draw in their boundaries, demanding that the appearance of the organization be preserved at all costs and that employees draw even closer together. Like the out-of-balance pyramid, as the circle contracts, it begins to control its members by requiring that they stay together, avoid conflict, and give the appearance of unity and agreement. Becoming either crooked or squishy is a response to a need for certainty. By contracting their shapes, organizations may appear to gain some security in tightening the boundaries that separate them from an uncertain world. Such security, however, is usually illusory.

The process of seeking a balance between pyramids and circles is one that is required by the forces of change. It requires that past behaviors be evaluated and new behaviors be established. In the process of evaluation a new course needs to be set, and those individuals who are active in the process will become the new leaders. Those who participate in the establishment of a new balance will move to the forefront of the organization. The mantle of leadership thus falls on those who can envision new directions - not on those who rigidify the directions of the past.

Opportunities in Turbulent Times

Security is not found in contraction, but in expansion and innovation. If people in organizations open themselves to new information about their environment and become more aware of current and forthcoming changes, they gain more information on which to base decisions about their future course. Pyramidal organizations that incorporate circles, and circular organizations that grow pyramids, will each have the increased flexibility with which to respond to crises in their environments. Thus the alternative offering the greatest chance of survival is not contraction but innovation, not closing in but opening up, not becoming crooked and squishy but relatively more upright and round both at the same time.

What this means is that individuals in pyramids, threatened by changes in their environment, will increase their effectiveness by welcoming and choosing from among the very ideas that are threatening to them. The changes that are instigated by the environment require that they adapt to this new environment, by incorporating many of the ideas that might have been foreign to them before. On the other hand, individuals in circles, bewildered by new demands for economic efficiency, may survive by considering some new structural alternatives, by reallocating power among hierarchical task forces, and balancing these new hierarchies with their traditional circles.

The process of seeking a balance between pyramids and circles is required by the forces of change. Past behaviors must be evaluated and new behaviors established. The process of choosing a future course, moreover, will give rise to new leadership. As new courses are selected, those who are willing to participate in their selection will move to the forefront of organizations. The mantle of leadership will fall on those who can create new directions - and not on those who rigidify the directions of the past.

The Process of Leadership

Those individuals excited about new opportunities to create functional balances within organizations are as excited about the process that is occurring as they are about the end product that might result. They are enthusiastic about what is going on at the moment and are not solely focusing on what the ultimate rewards will be. They love playing the game. In their ability to involve themselves in the present process, they are the ones who will shape the future. Those who adhere to the past and constrict their systems within rigid structures will wither away as the old yields to the new. Those who focus only on the future and the end product create another kind of rigidity, for they are constrained in the present by the boundaries of their future visions. They will never make it into the future that they envision, for they are not giving enough attention to the road that will lead them there.

Leaders have both vision and direction. They envision what may come and choose their directions in terms of their images of what will be. Once they do so, however, they focus on the process of getting there and give their attention primarily to the present, thriving on the immediate challenge. Ultimately, even though they have chosen the course and established the goals, they may end up being surprised at the results that do emerge. Happily, the results often exceed their expectations.

EXERCISE:
MINI-ORGANIZATIONAL EXPECTATIONS INVENTORY

Instructions: In the box or circle next to each statement, write a number from 1 to 4. In my organization this

        4 - always or almost always happens.
        3 - often happens.
        2 - occasionally happens.
        1 - rarely or never happens.

People are selected for jobs because they
- ▨ -know people in the organization
- ▨ -are friends with the boss
- ☐ -have essential skills
- ○ -can work within and shape the system
- ☐ -have the right credentials
- ○ -have growth potential

People are advanced in the organization because they
- ▨ -are willing to listen
- ☐ -agree with those in power
- ☐ -have privileged information
- ○ -create an effective network
- ▨ -are available at all times
- ○ -develop their own replacements

Approaches to planning include
- ▨ -never giving up on problems
- ☐ -spelling out duties in detail
- ▨ -everyone having a part in decisions
- ○ -establishing priorities
- ○ -seeking the best advice from all sources
- ☐ -one person making decisions

Organizational beliefs include
- ☐ -different leadership styles are accepted
- ☐ -everything must go through channels
- ☐ -tasks are assigned from the top
- ○ -diverse talents are used effectively
- ▨ -information is available to everybody
- ○ -people perform in areas where they do best

People want to work because they
- ▨ -enjoy being with others
- ▨ -want to keep their boss happy
- ☐ -want to get a better title
- ○ -want to make a contribution
- ☐ -enjoy being in charge
- ○ -want to make a contribution

Scoring:

To identify your perceptions of your organization, first add up all the numbers in the plain boxes. Then add up all the numbers in the shaded boxes. Subtract the plain box sum from the shaded box sum, multiply your answer by 2 and then divide by 5.

You perceive your organization as a Pyramid if you scored less than -2
You perceive your organization as a Circle if you scored more than +2
You perceive your organization as a Cone or combination of Pyramids and Circles if you scored between -2 and +2.

Then add up all the numbers in circles.

If your score is more than 30 you perceive your organization as effective
If your score is less than 20 you perceive your organization as ineffective
If your score is between 20 and 30 you perceive your organization as effective in some areas and ineffective in others

Four:
Players as Producers,
Integrators and Processors

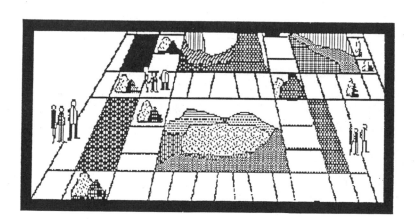

As the travelers continued along the squares moving in small bands towards the finish of the game, they not only wondered about the players who remained in either the hills or the valleys, but they wondered about themselves. Players in the hills were very good at doing things; those in the valleys spent more time sharing experiences with one another. Yet, among their own number, among the travelers, these same differences existed. Some of the travelers were better at doing things; some were better in working with the other players. In their small bands, the travelers with different skills often took different roles: some led the way in difficult terrain whereas others helped those who were stumbling over the rocky ground.

The travelers shared the same preferences and the same differences in skills that were apparent among those who remained in the hills and valleys . . .

The differences among people are strikingly evident to anyone observing any group of human beings at work or at play. Some people always walk slowly down the street; others rush, out of breath, to leave the current place behind. Some people arrive at new ideas while staring out the window, seated amid a clutter of papers and coffee cups, feet propped on the desk. Others are most productive when they sit intently in a quiet orderly office, feet on the floor, chair square to the desk. Most of us know managers who are loud and forceful and others who are warm and accepting. We know, too, many employees who are precise and punctual and others who are lackadaisical and impulsive. People, like organizations, come in many shapes and sizes.

Just as organizational structures differ among themselves, representing differing sets of rules and expectations, so too do people differ with varying sets of expectations existing within each individual. As we can sort organizational structures into pyramids and circles, as a greater handle for our understanding, so too we can sort people into rough categories, and gain a new framework for understanding differences. In recognizing differences, we acknowledge a variety of strengths which become the cornerstone for building a strong and flexible organization.

Players and Personalities

Just as many of the players on the gameboard have preferences for remaining in the hills or the valleys, so do we all have preferences for certain organizational settings over others. Some of us prefer to work in a pyramidal zone in which operations proceed in a logical, hierarchical fashion focused on getting things done. Others among us prefer to work in a circular zone in which operations are conducted in an intuitive, interactive modality focused on the exchange of information and personal experiences among all the players. Still others seek a balance between logic and intuition, hierarchy and interaction, pyramids and circles - finding themselves preferring neither circular nor pyramidal structures but rather the conical shape which combines the two. In structures shaped like cones we may focus both on getting things done and on sharing with others (see Figure 4.1).

Figure 4.1

CHARACTERISTICS OF PERSONALITY STYLES

	PRODUCERS (50%) 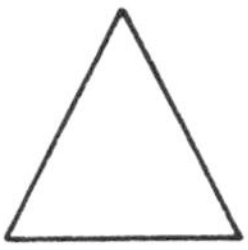	INTEGRATORS (35%) 	PROCESSORS (15%) 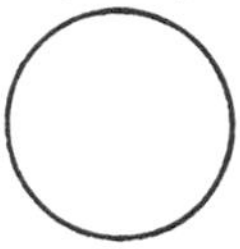
Primary focus of Attention:	Requirements of System	Requirements of System & Needs of Individual	Needs of Individual
Area of Creativity:	Products	Systems	Ideas
Response to Change:	Resistant	Moderately Open	Open
Willingness to Risk:	Low	Moderate	High
Style of Thought:	Logical	Logical & Intuitive	Intuitive
Preferred Activity:	Doing	Planning	Thinking

Those who prefer the rules and expectations of the pyramid to that of the cone and the circle are *Producers.* Producers, who make up the bulk of our population, assume that the world is shaped like a pyramid, with a few on top and many on the bottom. They base their behavior on this expectation. They respect the authority of those above them, and use their own authority to tell those beneath them what to do. They rely on logic and proven procedures. They sometimes believe that if all schedules, procedures, and timetables were clearly enforced, the world would be an efficient - and comfortable - place in which to live and work.

Those whose way of being is best suited to the circular structure are *Processors.* Processors make up only a small part of the population. They view the world as a circle, with everybody equally valuable to the functioning of the whole. They base their behavior on this world view. They tend to value the opinions of most people, and they often bypass the channels created by organizational authorities in order to share information with other individuals. They rely on intuition and sometimes ignore proven procedures. They believe that if all individuals were respected for their potential contributions, the world would be a warm - and productive - place in which to live and work.

Those preferring the zone between the circles and the pyramids, the conical zone, are the *Integrators.* Integrators make up approximately one third of the population - and the bulk of the managerial population. They view the world as an alternating landscape of pyramids and circles and, in their own behavior, seek to maintain a sometimes precarious balance between the two. They rely alternately on logic and intuition, being neither as logical as Producers nor as intuitive as Processors, and seek to bring the two together into a working balance. They tend to believe that maintaining a balance between individual contributions and established procedures will provide the greatest flexibility for an efficient and caring world.

Personality Styles and Organizations

Each of these personality styles - Producer, Processor, and Integrator - is necessary to maintain the effectiveness of an organization. Producers are *doers,* relatively content to carry out the routine business of the institution. Their relatively large numbers parallel the need for their orientation in maintaining the day-to-day effectiveness of any workplace. Producers are needed at almost all entry-level positions of organizations, and higher up in the accounting, engineering, and technical hierarchies.

Don Adamson is an example of a Producer. As a 55-year-old engineer, he is chief executive officer of a division of 5,000 salaried employees. His early years were spent in the navy, where he rapidly assumed positions of command. Training at Annapolis and the War College gave him a grasp of good managerial skills. He believed in making decisions at the top - but sharing them with his men. He believed in doing *his* job - which involved keeping his hand on the tiller - and in depending on his men to do theirs. Even as he maintained control, however, he spent a lot of time with his men - previously on board ship and now on the plant floor. "A good manager always visits his troops," was his byword.

Like many Producers, Mr. Adamson is not instinctively warm toward others - but he has learned he must share with others. He was not particularly receptive to others' ideas -

but he has learned to be fair and consistent and consequently does give his employees a hearing when they wish to talk to him. He treats his employees as equally as possible - holding them all to the same rules and regulations. Mr. Adamson is generally respected and admired by his employees. He has learned the rules of good management and holds himself to these rules, just as he holds others to those that apply to them.

Processors, in contrast, are *thinkers,* and prefer to spend their time generating ideas. Often limited to certain areas of organizations, they thrive on opportunities to create new ideas and envision new directions. Processors may be found at any time in higher-level positions in marketing, research, and training and development. There are relatively few entry-level positions for Processors and they must struggle through a "dues paying time" in their early career years before they are able to elect the positions in which they are most comfortable.

Take the case of Tom Barker who is a 45-year-old manager of an engineering unit. His upward rise as a young researcher had been stalled by his unwillingness to play by the rules of a large industrial company. Consequently, in mid-career, he was moved laterally to a managerial position over 65 men. Although this position entailed considerable responsibility, there were few chances of promotion and it was regarded internally as a *de facto* demotion. In managing his unit, Mr. Barker relies on his own sense of intuition. He responds to some of his employees more warmly than others, but he responds to all of them. He likes being with people, and in the early evening he can be found sitting in his own or a subordinate's office, reviewing the day - and possibly the fishing conditions for the next weekend.

Mr. Barker is a Processor. He is receptive to people, likes to discuss new ideas, and chooses to operate on "what feels right" at the moment. Conceptually he is in touch with the "big picture," but on a day-to-day basis he sees what and who is before him at the moment. Mr. Barker is both loved and hated. Those with whom he spends time love him. Others, who are unintentionally ignored in the rush of the day, hate him. They assume he is "out to get them." Rather, Mr. Barker simply hasn't run into them - nor thought of them - as he goes about his business. Although he tries to be consistent in his behavior with his subordinates, his good intentions generally fade away, and he lapses into companionable discussions with those whose offices adjoin his. At such times, he is likely to excuse his behavior by reminding himself that "consistency is the hobgoblin of small minds."

In stable times, the relatively small numbers of Processors have been more than sufficient for the needs of our organizations. They have often moved into the background when not engaged in work requiring generating new ideas, while others have run day-to-day operations. In today's unstable times, however, many Processors who have been in the back seat for years are moving forward into the driver's seat - in blazing new organizational trails and adventuring into the unknown. Whether their numbers will suffice for the need of the times is not known but certainly their talents will be utilized more fully than in a stable era.

Finally we come to Integrators, *planners* intent on building the structures for both Producers and Processors. They choose the present course utilizing lessons of the past and imagining possibilities for the future. In organizations, Integrators often move toward the top of any hierarchical system, because they delight in making things work from a systems perspective.

Renata Christensen exemplifies the Integrator's style. She is head of a troubleshooting unit for a worldwide manufacturing organization. She has just turned 40 and is one of the youngest people at her level in the entire corporation. Her rise in the company since she finished a master's degree (in an unrelated field) has been very rapid. She is highly thought of by all the people she works with, from the president of the corporation down to the hourly workers with whom she has come in contact.

Ms. Christensen is always aware of the overarching goal she has set for herself, namely working toward a better future for the organization as a whole. Yet, she balances the needs of individuals with those of the system. She understands the "big picture" of her corporation, but sometimes makes her decisions in light of pressing individual needs that come up suddenly.

Careful not to overcommit herself, she still sometimes finds herself tired and overworked. Her Integrator's style extends beyond the workplace into her personal life, where she is still seeking to balance her commitments in both worlds.

Players Responding to Change

Depending on their personality style, the players on the organizational gameboard respond differently to the winds of change. Producers are resistant to change as they are most comfortable in the patterns of yesterday. They respond to change by contracting rather than expanding. Fearful of losing what they have, they fail to focus on potentials for innovation. In times of change, Producers are most effective when protected from ambiguities by being given new, appropriate procedures and modes of operation. Guided through the process of change, without being forced to stretch their capacities beyond accustomed limits, Producers emerge again as the mainstays of their organization once it stabilizes.

Processors, on the other hand, come to the fore during times of change because they thrive on ambiguity and uncertainty. They view change as an opportunity for sloughing off the past and exploring an ever-promising future. Envisioning new worlds, they may outline the directions to be followed in times of turbulence and uncertainty, but still rely on others to actually plan the journey and draw up the maps. Then, having arrived at a new destination, they once again look toward the horizon as others focus on the task of building the present.

Integrators tread the path between Processors and Producers. Alive to new ideas, they also want to know if the ideas are viable. Aware of the benefits of past methods, they choose with care those that must go to make way for new directions. Integrators may be envisioned as building the bridges between past and future, between established procedures and new orientations, and creating the systems within which organizations and individuals may make the transitions from old to new. Not as resistant to change as Producers, nor as open as Processors, they carefully assess the costs and potential gains of both the past and future and create systems which operate most effectively in the present.

Adaptation and Growth

When times are uncertain, individuals do not have the choice of remaining comfortably in familiar patterns. Rather, they are offered two choices: to become less or more than they have been. In times of change, each personality style has a tendency to emphasize its own characteristics to the exclusion of others. In the face of change, personality styles tend to constrict and become more single-focused, just as pyramids tend to become more pyramidal (eventually becoming crooked) and circles more circular (eventually becoming squishy). Producers may retreat by emphasizing procedures. Integrators may retreat by emphasizing their own achievements. Processors may retreat into endless talk. Becoming more like one is already is the adaptive response to change, but in fact it becomes a choice to contract and become less than one is. This adaptive response ignores the possibilities available for developing new ways of being to suit the new environment.

The three personality styles can, on the other hand, choose to grow rather than contract in times of change: they can incorporate into their own behavior some of the strengths of the other styles. Producers can find a new satisfaction in increasing their awareness of others and learning to share in a team setting. Integrators can better use their talents and insight to help others (not only themselves) achieve, assuming responsibility for the direction in which many others may travel. Processors can move from interacting with others to focusing on achievement, putting their ability to talk to work and actually creating what they have been thinking about (see Figure 4.2.)

In the face of change, these choices are open. Individuals choose to expand or to contract based on the degree of individual insight and determination available to them as they choose, consciously or not, their personal response to change and uncertainty.

Figure 4.2

PERSONALITY STYLES AND RESPONSE TO CHANGE

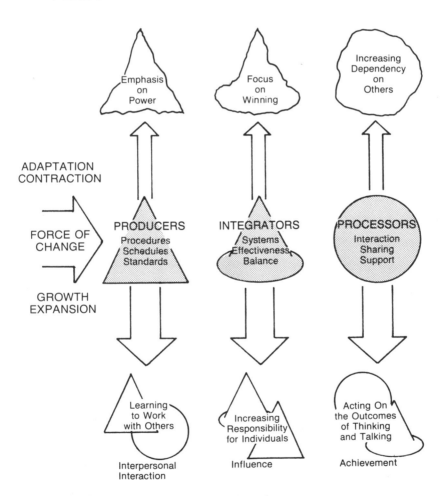

Players as Managers

Recognizing the choices open to different personality styles in times of turbulence and uncertainty, managers can help shape the course of their peers and subordinates. Knowing that Producers will become more effective by increasing their understanding of human relations, they may create circles for their Producer employees, encouraging them to share their concerns and problems with others. Aware too that Integrators will become most effective in positions of influence, they may allow their Integrator subordinates to exercise their growing managerial competencies with others within defined spheres. Finally, astute managers may encourage their Processor employees to leave talking behind and to achieve, by granting them the autonomy and providing the resources with which they can do so.

Another way to say the same thing is to talk about motivational strategies for each of three personality styles. Producers become more effective not when procedures are tightened and controls are imposed, but when they have an opportunity to work and share with others. Integrators increase their own scope not when they are left to their own individual achievements, but when they are given the chance to influence and take care of others. Finally, Processors achieve a higher level of effectiveness when they are led from talking about ideas to doing something about them, and to achieving at high levels.

Such motivational strategies can work in times of stability as well as in times of change. In stable times, however, individuals tend to follow the most comfortable road. Producers simply *do*, Integrators *plan*, and Processors *think*. In times of change, however, nothing is simple. Producers tend to increase the constraints existing within their power structure - unless they are led or lead themselves to focus on the needs of human individuals.   Processors tend to talk without conclusions - unless they learn to focus on getting things done in terms of individual achievement.   Finally, Integrators in such times tend to focus on individual achievement - unless they are encouraged to use their talents for the good of the entire system, taking responsibility for the functioning of the whole rather than the part.

The Opportunities of Change

Just as our organizational structures are required to become more than they are in times of change, so too are individuals - or they will inevitably become less. Change does not allow for a middle road. Individuals climb uphill or roll back down, because comfortable resting places are lost amidst earthquakes. Each style has its own growth direction. Each direction, moreover, leads to greater balance as individuals of each personality style incorporate some of the behaviors and some of the expectations of the other two.   In times of change, balance becomes a necessity.   Whether in organizational or individual systems, balance produces greater flexibility, which is better suited to changing circumstances. Moreover, in developing this flexibility, individuals and organizations not only adapt to change, but they shape the future emerging from an uncertain present.

EXERCISE:
MINI-PERSONALITY EXPECTATIONS INVENTORY

Instructions:

In the box next to each statement, write a number from 1 to 4. Mark your answers according to the following scale:

4- I almost always agree with this statement

3- I often agree with this statement

2- I occasionally agree with this statement

1- I rarely or never agree with this statement

☐ -You can't tell what others expect from you

▨ -The more you learn, the more there is to know

☐ -It's hard to know what others are thinking

☐ -One's associates usually think alike

▨ -Even in a group, people remain individuals

☐ -Too many points of view only lead to confusion

☐ -There is a right and a wrong way to do everything

☐ -When things go wrong, it's hard to understand why

☐ -It's difficult to try when people keep criticizing you

☐ -Some kinds of people just can't work together

▨ -Most people share some of the same feelings

☐ -Everybody is after the same thing

☐ -Everyone should know and follow the rules

☐ -There is only one good solution to any problem

▨ -The most important part of making a choice is accepting the consequences

▨ -It's enjoyable to meet and talk to new people

☐ -Others don't seem to understand me

▨ -Good problem solving requires hearing differences of opinion

☐ -There is no point in changing something that already works

☐ -It's good not to decide until you have all the facts

▨ -Careful analysis usually reveals a pattern

▨ -It's good to ask for help when you have a problem

☐ -There is little you can do to change the big things in life

☐ -First impressions are usually right

☐ -Conflict is best avoided

▨ -What each individual does makes a difference
☐ -Trusting others is dangerous
☐ -Good teams are made of similar kinds of people
▨ -It's good to hear different viewpoints when making a decision
☐ -They've either got it or they haven't
☐ -A good decision keeps all options open
▨ -Even good decisions need to be reevaluated over time
☐ -People who get ahead step on others
▨ -It's good to try out different ways of doing things
☐ -If it can't be done right, it's not worth doing
☐ -Ambition only reflects greed

Scoring:
To find your personality style, first add up all your numbers in the plain boxes. Then add up all your numbers in the shaded boxes. Subtract the plain box sum from the shaded box sum and divide your answer by 3.

You are probably a Producer if you scored less than -2.
You are probably a Processor if you scored more than +2.
You are probably an Integrator if you scored between -2 and +2.

(For further information on the interpretation of your scores see **Organizational Sync.**)

Five:
Players as Managers
and Leaders

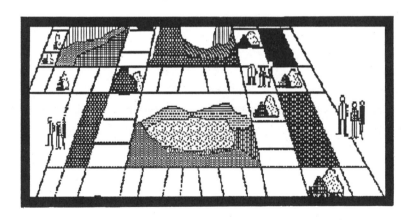

Sitting around the fire one evening, at the top of a stark and isolated cliff, the travelers wondered again about the differences among themselves, and the greater differences between themselves and those remaining back in the valleys and on the hills. What is it that they would tell the younger people just starting the game? How would they encourage them to go ahead of many others and to break new paths on the gameboard?

The travelers knew well that, accounting for their different sets of rules and different styles, almost all of the players managed well: some within each group informally set the stage for the others, assigning tasks and duties when necessary and making sure that all their people had food and shelter. Yet only among the travelers were there those who ventured forth into new territory . . . Why was this so? The answer, seemingly within grasp, continually eluded their reach.

Keeping one's hand on the tiller is a different activity than exploring a distant horizon. Maintaining one's course in the present is different from envisioning new lands in the future. In such ways do managers assume different functions from leaders. Managers make the most of the current situation, often seeing that goals are accomplished when it would appear that resources are inadequate for the purpose. As one executive joked, his talents would be superfluous if his unit had plenty of everything. Leaders, on the other hand, urge people on toward a future destination, encouraging them to leave familiar situations for unknown shores. Management requires the effective supervision of a work unit, no matter what size. Leadership requires the ability to envision, to make strategies, and to plan what work will be done years later - while establishing present goals in that context. Management and leadership are sometimes demonstrated by the same individuals - and sometimes not.

In times of change, both management and leadership become complex. The structures of organizations that are adapting to and expanding with turbulent conditions increase in complexity. Individuals motivated by the forces of change grow to new levels.

Managing in times of change requires managers to constantly keep in touch with current developments, to open up their own communication networks, and to reevaluate past designs in terms of present conditions. To lead in such a time requires not only establishing a firm base on shifting ground, but imagining the contours of the landscape in future times. To both manage and lead one must be quick on one's feet, and willing to live with uncertainty.

Players as Managers

Each personality style - Producer, Processor, and Integrator - has more or less ability to accommodate to uncertainty, and each has the ability to manage. The ways in which they manage, however, are different. Drawing on particular strengths, each personality style creates a different climate for subordinates within the organization. From different sets of expectations of the world, each personality style will cast a different management shadow, creating the employee's world within different outlines.

Yet just as the environment changes, so do managers change over time. Learning from experience, effective managers mature, creating a more balanced image of the world than when they began. They move from an early single-pointed focus to a more encompassing one, increasing their effectiveness as they do so. Mature managers develop the inner flexibility that allows them to manage effectively in a changing environment. From their numbers come the leaders of organizations who will cast their visions into the future, shaping what is to come.

Producers as Managers

Producers begin as managers by acting as *Chiefs* with reins of authority in their hands. They follow the directions of those above and expect that their own directions will be followed by those below them. They direct others through one-to-one confrontations, conferences, meetings, and memos. Their view of the world is such that there are few contingency plans for lack of compliance with directives from the top.

Art Hanson is a 55-year old supervisor who learned a long time ago that if you want people to do something, you tell them to do it. If they don't do it right away, you tell them louder. Consequently, Mr. Hanson has a reputation for barking at his men, and can often be heard throughout the floor of the plant in which he works. Nonetheless, his men respect him. Although they keep their distance, they know that Mr. Hanson will see that they always meet their production schedules - and that he treats them all in the same manner. There is an element of fairness in yelling at *everybody* and subjecting all to the same treatment. Mr. Hanson is a good example of the managerial style, *Chief*. He is a Producer, and operates at the first level of managerial development.

As producers mature, however, they become more benevolent and recognize the value of human interaction in making an operation work. They relate to their employees in a warm way - often as a father- or mother-figure. Thus the Chief often becomes the *Patriarch* or *Matriarch*, still insisting on rules and procedures but recognizing the need for making exceptions in individual circumstances. While the Patriarch or Matriarch still believes in a logical, hierarchical universe, he or she also understands that individuals need to receive support and assistance in a time of crisis. Like the head of a large family, the Patriarchal or Matriarchal Producer takes care of his or her own, through a practical perspective tempered by human understanding.

Tom Jacobs is a 32-year-old engineer in the testing division of a large industrial company. He is in charge of all the instruments used in testing and supervises a group of four other men. Although his superiors chide him for not seeing the "big picture," his men love him. He works closely with them, knows everything about instrumentation, and stands up for them in whatever situation occurs. He is warm and responsive to his men, but basically believes that good management is being consistent, fair, and getting the work done. He is unhappy that his unit is not managed in the same way he runs his own group - and that all standards and procedures are not enforced on a regular basis. He believes that if his unit manager would take the time to enforce the regulations, everyone would be more effective - and more satisfied.

Mr. Jacobs is a *Patriarch* in managerial style. His basic preference for rules and regulations has been supplemented by a genuine concern for "his people." He does not, however, step back and let them assume significant responsibility for themselves.

When the Patriarch/Matriarch is ready to mature to an even higher level of development, he or she adopts the role of *Clan Leader,* delegating responsibilities to other members of the clan who have earned that responsibility. Less involved in the nuts-and-bolts aspects of the work, the Clan Leader recognizes his or her own importance as a symbol to others. The Clan Leader upholds the emphasis on standards and procedures from afar, and may even take time out to pursue his or her own individual interests. Clan Leaders at this stage of development often have evolved their own particular hobbies or other pursuits, which do not compete with but complement the work experience. The distance thus created between the Clan Leader and the clan allows employees to take on more responsibility than with other managerial Producers.

With each level of managerial development, the Producer achieves a greater balance by incorporating more "circular" qualities. Initially most at home in pyramids, maturing Producers modify their styles so that pyramidal cones are their systems of preference. At higher levels of development Producers, still emphasizing procedures, still believing strongly in hierarchy, have become participative managers, allowing those beneath them to assume greater responsibilities for both decision making and implementation of procedures. The Clan Leader has developed a degree of flexibility for managing in uncertain times. (See Figure 5.1.)

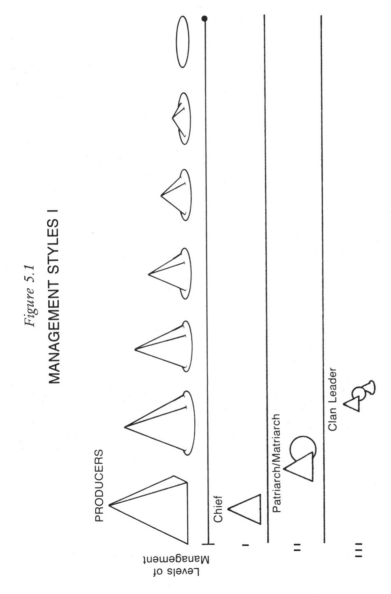

Figure 5.1

MANAGEMENT STYLES I

Processors as Managers

Managers who are processors begin with a set of values emphasizing the importance of interpersonal interaction among individuals; they focus on the morale of their people. Thus the young Processor begins as a *Counselor,* working on a one-to-one basis with employees, encouraging them to work through any personal difficulties so as to be able to devote themselves to their work. Available almost all the time, the junior Processor invites his or her employees to spend time visiting - and the employees generally do. However when decisions need to be made quickly and action must be taken, the beginning Processor is at a disadvantage. Never having emphasized rules, procedures, or chains of command, the tools for rapid movement are rarely available. Decisions are made slowly by individuals working together - sometimes three steps behind everybody else.

Jim Parkinson is the young assistant director of research for a new high technology company. He is charged with supervising much of the ongoing research of the firm and creating some of the procedures for detecting problems in new software packages. He can often be seen at his desk, feet propped up on the cluttered surface, smoking a cigarette and gazing out the window. When he gets down to work, however, he works intently and feverishly and will stay at the office into the night in order to complete a project or develop a new idea.

Mr. Parkinson is nonchalant, however, when asked about his management and supervision style. He has two subordinates who monitor the debugging of new programs and actually carry out the work that tests his ideas. "As long as they feel good about their work," he says, "I don't have to interfere much. One of them had some personal problems last week, and we spent several hours talking about them and working through his difficulties, and then we got back to work. I rarely do more than that." Mr. Parkinson's employees, however, much as they like him, often complain to each other that he neither gives clear enough directions nor tells them specifically what to do. Still, they feel very strongly about him and are willing to try and untangle any vague directions that come their way. Mr. Parkinson is a *Counselor,* a Processor at the first level of management development.

As Processors develop they increasingly accept the imperative of getting things done, along with some of the inequalities that necessarily occur when the focus becomes task-oriented. At this level, the Processor takes a new view of the managerial role and becomes a *Facilitator,* not only counseling and coaching others but encouraging them and demanding that they perform. Snags in performance schedules are sometimes still worked out on a one-to-one level, focusing on individual problems, but more often they are worked through in dealing with an entire group. The Facilitator, still believing in the worth of the individual, establishes an atmosphere in which people not only feel worthwhile but are encouraged to perform at the top of their abilities.

Susan Clark is a 35-year-old manager in the marketing division of a major corporation. Recently, she has taken on some of the training responsibilities for the corporation. She is personally very interested in the human relations side of training - in communication, teamwork and decision-making - and she has been instrumental in bringing programs connected with these topics into the company. When she succeeds in doing this she sits back, an interested observer, and takes satisfaction in having created an environment in which employees can learn and grow.

She is said, however, not to be as assertive as some other individuals in setting up the seminars for training. She believes that people should come to such sessions voluntarily and does little to insure that employees keep their initial commitments. Consequently, seminars set up by Ms. Clark are usually strong on supportiveness and openness, but a little "iffy" in terms of numbers of participants. Those who come benefit from the experience, but little is done to win over the recalcitrants. Ms. Clark is a *Facilitator* in management style, able to create growth-producing environments - and is willing to sit back and watch growth occur.

Only in full maturity does the Processor, basically focused on individuals, recognize the importance of systems. As the Processor develops and moves into larger arenas, dealing with more and more groups, the interrelationship of these groups becomes a major part of the Processor's world view. At this point, the Processor as manager becomes a skillful *Negotiator,* defining the rules and procedures by which groups interact. Rather than working with individuals alone, the Negotiator creates and monitors the systems by which groups of individuals can work with each other. Still in the background in a supportive role, the Negotiator is able to manage the complexities of large systems by developing ways in which subsystems can work with each other.

Each step of managerial development achieves a greater balance for the Processor. Starting at the other end of the management continuum than the Producer, the Processor as manager changes his or her preference for an entirely circular structure to that of a conical one in which circular and pyramidal qualities are combined. Still relatively flat, the development of the cone reflects the ability of highly developed Processors to get things done as well as to talk about it, to emphasize achievement and to standardize some rules as well as to focus on employee morale. The Negotiator has developed sufficient flexibility to manage a large system effectively and productively (see Figure 5.2.)

Integrators as Managers

Unlike the other two personality styles, the Integrator as manager begins in the middle of the management spectrum. The Integrator starts from a balanced position, with an awareness of the need for both pyramids and circles, of the need to both achieve and to work with others. The Integrator at this level, however, has little awareness of the need to influence others. Rather, relatively balanced within, the Integrator leaves management to itself and expects to run a system by example. Integrators at this level are *Role Models.* They will lead if others will follow, doing little, however, to insure that this occurs. Role Models take care of themselves and expect others to do likewise.

Aileen Danton is the newsroom manager for a local radio station. She has been at the job for ten years. Her work has always been superb, and over the years she has tied up more and more of her life in her job. Recently, changes at the top of the national corporation necessitated some changes in supervision at the radio station. The general manager, an easygoing fellow, was replaced by a new man who felt insecure in his position and began tightening the rules. This new general manager then took one of the staff from the newsroom and elevated him to project director - making him

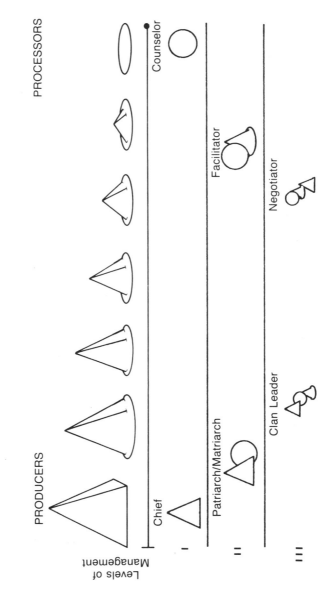

Figure 5.2

MANAGEMENT STYLES II

Ms. Danton's immediate supervisor.

The project director, Tony Bartholomew, gave little credit to Ms. Danton, for he wanted to make this *his* operation. He discounted her work and asked her instead what she had done for her people. He wanted accountings of time, projects, and accomplishments for the last year. Ms. Danton had led her unit in the past by focusing on her own work and by being best at what she did. Her subordinates learned to do their own work by watching and modeling her.

Ms. Danton had successfully used the style of *Role Model* until the arrival of Tony Bartholomew. Now, her job was in jeopardy for she had managed by example, rather than by supervision of schedules and procedures, and she did not have the records to give to her new supervisor. Although her unit turned toward collecting this data, Ms. Danton was bitter and unhappy. In the past, her work had been most important - and her staff had worked, without supervision, right along with her. To shift her focus to their work, to encourage them to achieve and limit her own achievement, were not part of her managerial expectations. She was still at the first developmental level, the Integrator as Role Model.

At the next level of development, however, Integrators realize that all people are not alike, that setting examples is insufficient, and that it is necessary to assume some responsibility for the awareness and performance of others. At this stage, Integrators become *Team Leaders,* using their influence to move others toward common goals. Changing the primary pronoun from "I" to "we," Integrators now work with others to encourage them to achieve. Less focused on individual achievement (what *I* can do), Integrators become effective as group leaders focusing on group achievement (what *we* can do). Establishing procedures and showing support, effective

Team Leaders move their groups down the field to the final goal.

Paul Edwards is about to be promoted to principal engineer, in charge of seven other engineers. He has worked successfully in a lesser position, primarily alone, for the last four years. His ability to get his work done effectively and to get along with his boss and the current principal engineer have led to his imminent promotion. Mr. Edwards is one of the few men in the unit who is able to recognize the talents of other individuals at the same time as he understands the constraints of the system. He has a good deal of "organizational sense" as well as technical competence. Yet, in the last four years his efforts have focused on making his own work excellent. His boss is worried that he may not fully understand that he can no longer manage by example. But Mr. Edwards is, in fact, beginning to see that he must enlarge his picture of management as he moves into a new role as Team Leader, recognizing and using the individual strengths of his men, while respecting their limitations. Although somewhat reluctant to do so, he is becoming increasingly ready to focus his attention on helping others to achieve -- and less on his own efforts.

At even higher levels, Integrators learn to be *Systems Coordinators,* creating the rules and procedures that will help many groups achieve their own goals within the boundaries of the larger system. Intent on building a functioning system, the Systems Coordinator will establish the procedures that allow all units to function well. Taking less of an upfront position than the Producer, and less of a back seat than the Processor, the Systems Coordinator stands in between, building the master plan that will let each group work productively and satisfactorily.

The Integrator begins with a modicum of balance, poised between the two ends of the continuum. Yet this Integrator, like other beginners, still has a narrower vision than is necessary for full effectiveness. The balance reflected by the early Integrator is an inner balance, focused on self. With experience and maturity, the Integrator learns to acknowledge first systems and second group differences within those systems, developing a balance that includes not just self but others - and the larger world. The experienced Systems Coordinator has achieved a new level of balance, encompassing larger and larger arenas, that brings much more perspective to his or her managerial view than that of the beginning Integrator. The system of preference for the Systems Coordinator is thus nearly centered on the pyramidal-circular continuum but leans slightly toward the end of encouraging others do for themselves what they can best do (see Figure 5.3.)

Achieving a Balance on the Gameboard

Effective management makes the best use of both material and human resources, thus achieving maximum output from minimum input. In order to do this in times of uncertainty, communication lines must be open, decision-making structures must be established, and people at the top must have the good judgement to choose the most likely course for achieving both productivity and satisfaction. People at the top exhibit all personality styles, depending on the nature of the unit and the organization. Although Integrators predominate in these positions, Producers and Processors find themselves there as well.

Figure 5.3

MANAGEMENT STYLES III

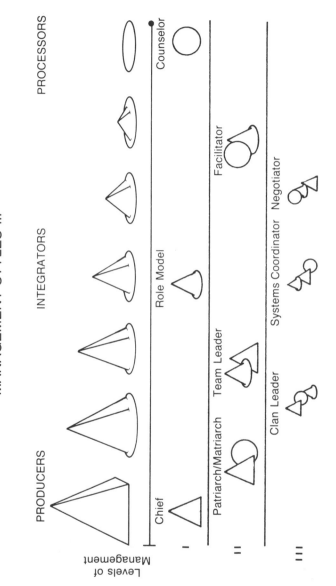

It is imperative that these managerial players be able to recognize the importance both of the individual and the system, harnessing both individual and systems resources to achieve organizational goals. This can happen only when a balance between human needs and task priorities is established, when individuals are open to new alternatives for action and are capable of selecting the most appropriate one.

All managers at lower levels of development have difficulty doing this, as each is focused on only a limited area of the management spectrum. Early Producers see procedures, Integrators see personal achievement, and Processors see employee morale. However, as each style progresses in experience and maturity, each develops a greater breadth of vision. Each is able to integrate the needs of people and tasks within the larger system. Yet each retains its earlier focus, blending it with a comprehensive understanding of organizational life.

Moving into Leadership

To manage, however, is not the same as to lead. To lead in times of uncertainty requires the ability to envision new worlds, to develop strategies for bringing those into being, and to design the plans that will detail the steps along the way. To lead is to develop the ways through which the present can become a particular vision of the future. Individuals who are able to lead will do this in many ways, in accord with their basic tendencies. Some may provide the vision by pointing out the new worlds as yet unseen over the horizon, others may choose the course by which we might get there, and others may actually chart the course by which we make our way.

The act of leadership requires all three capabilities, often found in different people. The act of leadership, therefore, is often a team effort.

We are defining leadership styles as distinct from management styles. Some small proportion of managers (whether Processors, Integrators or Producers) actually become leaders (see Figure 5.4). Those who do have their own particular leadership style, and each contributes one important and distinctive aspect to the total leadership endeavor. Some become *Visionaries* and set the broad outlines for future directions. Others become *Strategists* and select the paths by which these directions may be best pursued. Still others are *Designers,* filling in step by step the pathways of the new directions. All three leadership styles look toward the future and connect the future with the present. All three, however, bring to the act of leadership a different skill with which to shape what is to come.

Throughout history, we have given most credit to the Visionaries - for example Thomas Jefferson, Abraham Lincoln, Albert Einstein, Albert Schweitzer. Strategists appear in history books most often in military and political realms, with such figures as George Washington and Dwight Eisenhower (as general, not president) heading the list. Of Designers we know less though Harry S. Truman and Henry Ford are good candidates for this leadership style (even though they overlap some with strategists).

Every Designer follows in the steps of Strategists and Visionaries who have outlined new directions, and every Visionary needs a number of Strategists and Designers behind him or her, able to implement the outlines of a new world. In each act of leadership, all three styles are essential. Each contributes to the whole.

Figure 5.4

MANAGEMENT AND LEADERSHIP STYLES

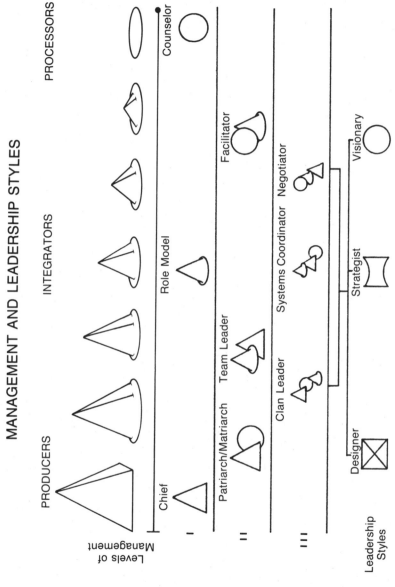

To Manage and To Lead

In times of uncertainty, all individuals with the ability to work with others have a responsibility to use their talents both to manage and to lead, to take care of the present even as they look toward the future. They may do so in informal or formal ways, from positions of minimal authority to those of high authority. In each case, such individuals will be most effective when they seek a balanced vision of what is and what can be - and develop the inner flexibility to adapt and shape the forces of change.

EXERCISE:
MINI-ORGANIZATIONAL PROBLEM-SOLVING INVENTORY

Instructions: In the box next to each statement write a number from 1 to 4 in accord with the following scale:

4- I almost always agree with this statement
3- I often agree with this statement
2- I occasionally agree with this statement
1- I rarely or never agree with this statement

☐ -The causes of most problems can be clearly isolated and defined in concrete terms

▨ -Even small changes may have great effects

☐ -The worth of any project can be measured in dollars and cents

☐ -Good projects involve low risk to individuals and short-term rewards

▨ -Sometimes strange or unusual solutions to problems may have a better probability of success than standard practices

☐ -The best way to resolve problems will minimize risk to all involved

☐ -Worthwhile solutions to problems will necessarily have visible and positive short-run consequences

☐ -Each step of an action plan must be completed on schedule for the project to be successful

☐ -Most problems can be explained in simple, easily understood language

☐ -Major organizations' problems can generally be resolved by increasing or improving technological resources

▨ -Sometimes the best solutions to problems require high commitments of time and energy from everybody involved

☐ -Any project that can actually be completed is significant

☐ -The value of any project should be self-evident, so that little time is wasted persuading others of its worth

▨ -Action plans must be flexible to account for unpredictable happenings in human lives

☐ -Work teams made up of ordinary people cannot expect extraordinary results

☐ -A good solution easily wins the approval of those involved

☐ -Outcomes that cannot be easily measured have no place in action plans

▨ -Problems can often be best stated in terms of parables or other symbolic communication

▨ -The best solution may be arrived at as a result of insight rather than logic

☐ -Individuals will invest time and energy only in projects that offer them tangible rewards

▨ -Some worthwhile projects require more personal risk with less likelihood of personal gain

☐ -Problems that occurred in the past have little to do with what is happening now

☐ -Considering more than three alternative solutions to a problem is generally a waste of time

▨ -A problem is often only a symptom of a more serious underlying difficulty in human relationships

Scoring:
To find your problem-solving (leadership) style, first add up all the numbers in the plain boxes. Then add up all the numbers in the shaded boxes. Subtract the plain box sum from the shaded box sum and divide your answer by 2.

You are probably a Designer if you scored less than -2.
You are probably a Visionary if you scored more than +2.
You are probably a Strategist if you scored between -2 and +2.

Six:
Players in Pyramidal
and
Circular Groups

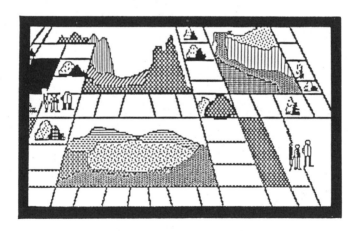

In the hills of the organizational gameboard, players lived as if in pyramids with an emphasis on the evaluation and use of skills in order to get the work done. In the valleys, on the other hand, circles were the order of the day and players focused on the need to accept information from all of their kind before arriving at a decision. In the valleys and on the hills, the players followed different sets of unspoken rules, always working with the others who believed the same as they . . .

Americans think of themselves as individuals first and group members second: they believe that they do most things by themselves and that achievement is the result of one person's skill and effort. The cultural history of America emphasizes the individual and Americans consequently perceive the organizational landscape peopled by individuals, usually in isolation from each other. A truer picture would be to view the landscape dotted with many groups of interconnected individuals - proceeding together on various organizational gameboards. Our belief in independence has caused us to slight the real interdependence of individuals with each other - and with a larger system composed of many groups.

Despite the fact that many of us believe in the importance of the individual over the group, most of us acknowledge that we spend most of our time in company with others. For example, a group of manufacturing supervisors and managers from a variety of plants recently estimated that they spend between 90 and 99 percent of their work time with other people. The longest uninterrupted period of time they had experienced in the last two weeks at work was one hour, but the average amount of uninterrupted time they experienced for the last two weeks was between five and ten minutes. This group of managers is typical of managers and supervisors in general. Most managerial time is spent in the company of others, either in groups, on a one-to-one basis, or on the telephone. Thus most managerial time is spent talking or listening to others, with little time spent alone or in independent activity.

Despite the fact that management is a group activity, much of our thinking about managers and management has focused on the individual. We are just beginning to admit that management is a group activity, and that the ability to work well with others is the key to managerial effectiveness. As individuals in corporations are becoming more aware of the importance of group activity, each is asking the obvious questions: Given that I spend most of my time with others, and that I am going to spend even more of my life in the company of others, how do I make this time productive, how do I make it count? The increased awareness of the centrality of group activity in organizations has appropriately focused attention on the ineffectiveness of many group encounters. The effectiveness of group activity is one of the most important factors in improving use of our human resources - and, hence, increasing our productivity. Stretching a bit, one might suggest that the efficacy of group interaction is at the root of organizational survival.

Pyramidal and Circular Groups

Any group of individuals together for any length of time begins to take on a shape of its own, determined by the patterns of human interaction that become established within the group. The shapes established by these patterns of interaction may be described as relatively pyramidal or circular. Just as larger organizations tend to develop a hierarchy or lie flat against the ground, so do all smaller groups. Thus, effective groups will either have a recognized leader who respects and accepts all group members, or they will be primarily leaderless, with each member performing a relatively equal and valued function within the group. However, most groups do not assume absolute forms. Rather, pyramidal groups have an identifiable leader who sometimes interacts on a peer level with other members of the group, and circular groups often have a leader who, for a limited time, takes responsibility for the decisions and actions of the group. Still, groups may be identified as primarily pyramidal or circular.

Ineffective groups are similar to crooked pyramids and squishy circles. Within a small group as well as a large one, one member may dominate others, creating resentment, hostility, and/or apathy among group members. Small groups, nominally without a leader, may cling together to repel outside forces, limiting their own autonomy and their openness to new information. The boss as tyrant is a symbol of the crooked pyramid. The interminable, do-nothing meeting is a symbol of the squishy circle.

With a new awareness of the importance of group activity in organizations, it is imperative that we learn to discriminate between effective and ineffective groups, and to turn the latter into the former. In learning to work together in organizations, we move one step closer to economic survival and productivity.

Work Groups as Pyramids

Pyramidal work groups are often composed of natural work teams that include a boss and several subordinates, or they are brought together as a specific task force to focus on one issue. Pyramidal groups are designed to get things done and to accomplish specific tasks. They are designed as mini-hierarchies with a leader and several followers, although the followers may vary in rank, some assuming various degrees of leadership themselves. Psychologically, effective pyramidal work groups result in higher self-esteem for each member, based on a sense of accomplishment. In terms of structure, effective pyramids occur most often when the formal leader of the group (according to the organizational chart) also has the informal power to actually lead the group.

Generally, we tend to imagine a small pyramidal group operating in an either-or fashion. Either it is functioning smoothly, with directions flowing downward, respect beaming upward, and work output the result (see Figure 6.1), or we view the mini-pyramid as a scene of tension and resentment with crises provoking an uneven work flow (see Figure 6.2). We visualize either the ideal, a harmonious group, with everybody having the same understanding of functions and goals, or we imagine the worst, a stress-ridden group in which all members take care of their own interests at the expense of the others. Contrasting with these expectations, the reality -- and the basis for effectiveness -- might be found in between.

Figure 6.1

THE IDEA OF A PYRAMIDAL TEAM

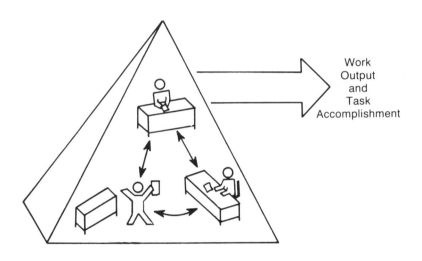

A set of expectations leading to productivity in pyramidal groups recognizes individual differences. The ways in which the boss operates may be different from those of subordinates, and each subordinate may be different in his or her own way. The boss may be a Producer, a rules-and-procedures woman, and the subordinate may be an Integrator, interested

Figure 6.2

THE REALITY OF A PYRAMIDAL TEAM

in running the show. Or the boss may be a Processor, a man focused on morale and individual satisfaction, and the subordinate may be a Producer, wanting to know what to do and when to do it rather than focusing on interpersonal interaction. In each case, people in groups become more effective as they recognize and accept the differing styles of others.

Realistic expectations regarding different situations also further a productive and effective work effort by a pyramidal group. Some situations require rapid action - and a decision by the boss in order to meet time deadlines and to focus the productivity of the entire team. Some situations require decisions made periodically over time, so that ultimate decisions will be based on as much information as possible. Individuals adapt to both situations more easily when they expect that both will occur - and that neither is the creation of another individual so much as a result of living in a changing environment.

Within pyramids then, people who recognize the effects of both individual and situational differences, increase their effectiveness by aligning responsibilities with individual strengths and environmental demands. Exact job descriptions may be altered slightly in order to give individuals the work assignments most suited to their talents. The rules-and-procedures boss may recognize the need for some responsibility on the part of her subordinates and allow them to manage specific projects while she maintains the schedules and the procedural uniformity. The manager focused on morale may spend time coaching employees and encouraging others in the group to formulate the rules, procedures, and timetables for task accomplishment. In a sense, each work group is unique, and work patterns that are tailored to each particular group increase effectiveness.

In other words, when we give up our expectations that work groups function just alike from one situation to another, and that individuals within each group perform in similar ways, we align our expectations more closely with reality. Realistic expectations regarding work groups become the basis for an effective unit.

In the following example the work group alternated between being a moderately effective pyramid - when the boss gave directions - and a squishy circle - when his subordinates took over in order to protect one of their incompetent members. Given the temperament of the people in this group, and the tasks they had to accomplish, the goal was to increase effectiveness by turning it into an upright pyramid.

The boss was a general supervisor who oversaw the work of three shift supervisors. He was a competent, thoughtful man who held himself and his unit to very high expectations. As a consequence of expecting so much he was often disappointed and frustrated, but accepted this wryly as part of life. He often stepped back and let things take their course, allowing his supervisors to set directions and see that the work was done.

These supervisors varied in ability: one was very good with people but a little too easygoing; another was a grumpy, white-haired man who "chewed out" the men frequently but knew what he was doing technically; and the third was largely incompetent but covered for by the other two. The first supervisor, the easy-going one, got most of the work done but let his people take long lunch breaks and leave early. The second one, the "grumpy" technical expert, was relied on for his knowledge but found himself complaining and yelling all the time to little avail. The third incompetent one did little and hid his deficiencies behind the work of the other two.

The general supervisor wanted to improve the record of the unit but initially saw only two choices: go on as they were or take his frustrations out on his men, in which case he knew the supervisors would band more tightly together and take over direction of the unit all the time instead of just part of the time. It did not occur to him that opening up discussions with his subordinates, the supervisors, might, in fact, be one route to strengthening this unit. When it was pointed out to him that, indeed, if he were perceived by his men as more open to their ideas and a better listener, they might be able to put their different styles and abilities on the table and together seek a way of improving their output, he was willing to give it a try. Once the problem of covering for the less competent supervisor was in the open, they might all work together to either improve his capabilities, lessen his work load, or assist with whatever other problems were hindering his performance.

The unit as a whole has decided to deal with the differences in ability among the three shift supervisors, and is committed to aligning its expectations about individual responsibilities with the reality of individual styles and abilities. Whether or not the unit will become an upright, well-functioning pyramid is still to be seen.

Another unit was struggling with the problem of being a squishy circle. The top management team of this unit was headed by Gerald Black, a warm friendly man who liked to talk with his men, was vague in his directions to them and often called them down for not doing what he expected - which he had never clearly communicated in the first place. Next in command was John Fallaway, an idealistic, unambitious thinker. His main charge was the day-to-day supervision of the unit. He paid so little attention, in general, to these activities that his supervision was haphazard and perceived as uncaring. He was accused of playing favorites and playing politics.

The two men at the next level down were both more dynamic than Mr. Fallaway. Carl Thomas was a forthright, sturdy man who believed in more work and less talk, and withdrew from management team discussions to attend to day-to-day business details. Martin Moore, already picked to move upward the fastest, was a competent, intelligent, and warm person but overly aggressive in his contacts with others. Mr. Moore continually tried to move the unit in a positive (according to him) direction, and resorted to bulldozing his way through when agreement was not forthcoming. His relatively low status prevented him from being successful in his efforts to get his way through authoritative statements. Power in this unit, centered at the bottom and shared by both Mr. Thomas and particularly Mr. Moore, labeled the unit a circle. The ineffectiveness of either man in persuading the unit to move in directions they believed appropriate led to Mr. Thomas's withdrawal and Mr. Moore's aggression.

A change in the formal structure which, with the blessing of Mr. Thomas, increased Mr. Moore's status and removed Mr. Fallaway from the supervisory scene, has created an effective pyramid with Mr. Moore in charge. His opinions are now adhered to by the others. The boss, Mr. Black, is now free to talk and generate ideas with his men, knowing that the unit is being run effectively by his immediate subordinate.

Work Groups as Circles

Circular work groups often develop from peer groups, sometimes for overtly social purposes, or they may be brought together as committees or problem-solving groups. The most common setting for the circle is the conference room of the organization. Circular groups are designed to share information and generate ideas around problem situations. They are flat in nature, assuming equality among members *at that moment in time.* Psychologically, effective circular work groups result in increased self-esteem, based on a sense of belonging and involvement in the decision-making process.

Just as with pyramidal groups, circular groups are often incorrectly viewed in an either-or fashion. We commonly have an idea that all members of a circular group share a similar purpose, are well prepared for a meeting, and are interested in and attentive to the group process. We reveal

Figure 6.3

THE IDEA OF A CIRCULAR TEAM

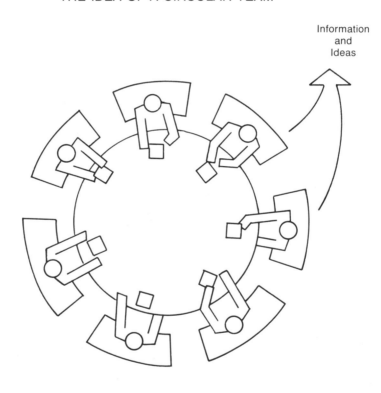

Information
and
Ideas

our belief in this idea whenever we complain that so-and-so is not doing his or her share. Group members' complaints about each other are a frequent part of much group functioning, and suggest that members expect that circular groups (committee meetings, discussion groups, and so forth) are composed entirely of people equally prepared, who can then generate an uninterrupted flow of ideas and alternatives for solving problems (see Figure 6.3). When this idea proves false, and members do not contribute relatively equally to this process, a different scenario quite often occurs in which some people run the show and others retreat in apathy or resentment (see Figure 6.4).

Again, the reality lies in-between. With the acceptance that different individuals make different contributions, we have more realistic expectations, and the basis for developing an effective circular group. Informally, the group may draw upon various individual strengths. Producers, for example, may be relied upon for monitoring procedures, and Processors for their social ease and occasional insight. Integrators may provide the structure that holds the group together and focuses attention on the goals and purposes of the unit.

In circular as in pyramidal groups, the shape of the group must also adapt to situational as well as individual differences. Occasionally the group may have no pressing concerns and be relaxed and sociable. At other times, urgent matters may either distract the attention of some members or focus them intensely on the subject matter under discussion. A recognition of variations in situation, as well as in personality styles, is essential for effective group functioning.

In the next two examples two work groups moved from squishy circles to round circles. Personality and situational

Figure 6.4

THE REALITY OF A CIRCULAR TEAM

Information

and

Ideas

variables made it unlikely that either would function well as a pyramid; consequently, the circle was the appropriate structure.

In a similar supervisory unit to the one described above, in the same company but in another department, a group of three shift supervisors and a general supervisor were functioning ineffectively - rather like a squishy circle. The three shift supervisors had all been there quite a long time, longer than their superior. They were all relatively powerful and respected by their men. One among them was regarded as an expert in human relations, another an expert in technical areas, the third was generally the mediator when debates arose. The general supervisor had entered this unit when the shift supervisors had been functioning together for over three or four years, expecting to assume command of the unit and to issue orders. His orders, however, were generally ignored and the team of three shift supervisors continued to run the show. The squishiness of their circle came from the fact that informally the shift supervisors deliberately - and with some effort - managed to exclude their boss from any decision-making function.

It was unlikely that this group would turn itself into an effective pyramid, with the boss assuming both formal and informal leadership while the supervisors became followers. The supervisors had already established their competence and ability to run the unit in the previous years - newer to the unit the boss had much to learn from them. Therefore, it seemed likely that this particular unit might more easily turn into a round circle in which all share in the decision-making process on an informal level. After several months of training the unit did in fact become an effective circle. The boss relinquished his hope of supreme power and agreed to join his men in a semi-peer-level relationship. The team of three benefitted from acknowledging the input of the boss, for although they shared much competence among them, none had the ability to be clear and decisive in setting expectations for themselves and each other. Thus a decisive voice was added to their pool of team talent, which already included skills in human relations, mediation and technical areas. The improved effectiveness of this supervisory team was documented in evaluations by their subordinates. This team now operates as an effective circle.

A second example occurred during the course of a three-day management development seminar in which one work group acted first as a crooked pyramid and then became a round circle. In initial problem-solving sessions George Paxton, the plant manager, dominated conversation. The superintendent and assistant superintendent, both competent and able men, hunched over in their chairs and acceded to the direction set by Mr. Paxton. The superintendent later said that he was so seething with resentment that he was afraid to open his mouth for fear of what might come out. The assistant superintendent said he was often either silent or angry in such situations and chose silence as the better alternative. The plant manager, Mr. Paxton, was totally unaware of their feelings and assumed the discussion and decision had been the choice of the entire group.

Two days later, after extensive discussion of his behavior aided by videotape feedback, Mr. Paxton was able to turn his strength from domination to responsive guidance of the group process. Biting his lip at times to keep from leaping into the fray with his own opinions, he created an atmosphere in which all members of the group offered and discussed opinions. The superintendent emerged as a strong, responsive leader able to side with the plant manager. The assistant superintendent offered his opinions without anger but with firmness. Other members of the group said it was the best discussion that they had ever had with their work team. In exercising great restraint, plant management discovered new alliances and new strengths among colleagues. The personal power previously used to dominate and create a crooked pyramid had been channeled into firmness and responsiveness, and the result was an effective circle.

Alternating Pyramids and Circles

Most individuals in organizations operate in both pyramidal and circular groups - and improve their own effectiveness when they can demonstrate the behaviors that are appropriate to the particular group they happen to be in at a given time. A task-centered orientation and acceptance of a hierarchical chain of command is appropriate for the pyramidal setting. A people-centered orientation and responsiveness to the ideas of all members is appropriate for a circular setting. To the degree that individuals develop a repertoire of behaviors appropriate for both settings, they increase their own flexibility and effectiveness in the face of changing circumstances.

Groups too, whether pyramidal or circular, increase their effectiveness by maintaining their flexibility. The shape of the group may change to meet the requirements of conditions existing both inside and outside the group. Formal or informal roles may be designed to make the most of individual strengths. The pyramidal or circular nature of the group may shift to meet demands for task accomplishment or problem solving. Groups that fail to maintain this flexibility become rigid and impermeable over time. Pyramids that fail to become circles from time to time will remain closed to new ideas, and circles that fail to become pyramids once in a while will lose the opportunity to implement ideas. In a structural sense, then, as in the individual sense, the key to effectiveness is flexibility.

Effective groups, therefore, are flexible in assigning roles to group members and in adopting the overall structure most suited to the situation at hand. As we turn now to the actual process that occurs in groups, we will shift our focus from personality styles and system structures to the impact of communication and expectations within and among groups. The interaction that makes a group a group is the communication among individuals. The foundation for much of this communication rests on the expectations of group members, otherwise known as group norms. Both communication and group norms will be examined in the following chapters. When communication is clear and group norms are constructive, most work groups operate effectively as upright pyramids and round circles, with structures alternating with each other to best fit the individuals and the situation.

EXERCISE: MINI-GROUP PERCEPTIONS INVENTORY

Instructions:

In the box next to each statement, write a number from 1 to 4 indicating your perception of members of your work group by completing the sentence: I perceive members of my work group as . . .

        4- almost always this way
        3- often this way
        2- occasionally this way
        1- rarely or never this way

☐ -Unwilling to share personal experiences with others

▨ -Interested in discovering the patterns reflected in different viewpoints

☐ -Convinced that once a project is set in motion the direction cannot be changed

▨ -Of the opinion that even good decisions need to be re-evaluated in time

▨ -Supportive of other individuals in the face of setbacks

☐ -Careful to leave before an argument begins

☐ -Given to making snap judgments about others
☐ -Reluctant to identify with common goals
☐ -Likely to avoid dealing with specific issues
☐ -Likely to make the same decisions over and over again
☐ -Continually seeking approval and agreement
☐ -Certain that luck is a critical factor in achieving anything
▨ -Open to alternative ways of accomplishing tasks
☐ -Not interested in why people believe as they do
▨ -Willing to recognize and appreciate individual differences
☐ -Careful to keep one step ahead of other people
▨ -Likely to consider the feelings of others in most situations
☐ -Most concerned about how things 'ought' to be done
▨ -Reluctant to make final judgments on surface impressions
☐ -Reluctant to make changes in daily routine
▨ -Able to change old beliefs to fit current experiences
☐ -Likely to take rumors about us or one of us seriously
☐ -Confused about the differences between peoples' opinions and what's really happening
☐ -Willing to let other people take care of the details
☐ -Convinced that success has little to do with individual effort
▨ -Unwilling to see any matter as completely closed
☐ -Reluctant to change something that already works
☐ -Not likely to be aware of current trends
▨ -Open to sharing group rewards with all individuals
☐ -Willing to give up when there are no immediate rewards
☐ -Convinced that one person's success is paid for by others
▨ -Open to appreciating people for their unique qualities
☐ -Opposed to seeing another person's point of view
☐ -Uneasy with any decision that upsets people
▨ -Likely to direct conflict toward achieving a creative solution
☐ -Reluctant to arrive at any decision of consequence

Scoring:

To find the personality style of members of your work group - as you perceive them, first add up all the numbers in the plain boxes. Then add up all the numbers in the shaded boxes. Subtract the plain box sum from the shaded box sum and divide your answer by 3.

Your group is probably made up largely of Producers who operate best in Pyramids if your score is less than -2.

Your group is probably made up largely of Processors who operate best in Circles if your score is more than +2

Your group is probably made up largely of Integrators who operate best in Cones if your score is between -2 and +2.

Seven:
Rules of Communication
on the
Gameboard

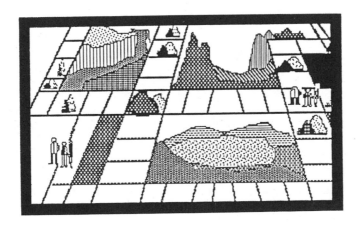

Those in the hills are good workers. They play to work on the organizational gameboard. When they talk to each other, not as often as one might think, they are clear in establishing expectations about how to accomplish the task. They are also clear in evaluating the performance of each other in accomplishing the task. "This is good," and "this is bad," are frequent phrases in the hills, almost as frequent as "this is right," and "this is wrong." The fact that these players are clear in telling others what they think does not mean, however, that others listen to what is said. When there are snarl-ups in the work in the hills, it has been said that the problems occur because nobody is listening.

People in the valleys provide a marked contrast. In the valleys people listen to each other. Yes, they share their experiences with others of their group, but sometimes they withhold information because they do not want to offend anyone. When some players are negligent in some area or another, for example, the other players are careful not to comment on this delinquency. They avoid hurting the feelings of others and, in such cases, do not say what they mean. Consequently, when things don't go well in the valleys, which happens from time to time, it has been said that the problem is that nobody will tell anybody anything. Such is the way of the valleys.

Most managers know that good communication is critically important. They recognize that in spending over 90% of their time with others, they are spending this time *talking* and *listening* to other people. How effective they are in their jobs, how productive are their units, depends on how well people talk and listen to each other. Further, the people who talk and listen best often become the leaders of the group or the organizations. They know what they think and are able to tell others, and also listen to others' opinions. Thus they are open to themselves and to their organization, and are able to gather the information on which to base effective decisions.

Everything in an organization, therefore, rests on the links of communication between people. Effective communication is the process through which people and groups knit themselves together, and ineffective communication is the way in which any threads that connect one person with another may be unraveled. When communication between individuals is effective, group interaction generally results in productivity and satisfaction for group members. When communication between individuals is ineffective, group interaction may result in lowered productivity and satisfaction.

There are rules which distinguish good from poor communication. Anybody can observe - or learn to observe - how well individuals follow these rules by watching and listening to nonverbal and verbal patterns of behavior. As people talk, move, gesture, turn away from or lean toward others, they reveal what they think of themselves and the group. People who work together over time establish patterns of behavior which remain fairly constant. For each long-term set of associations, in fact, these constancies take on the shape of a mini-pyramid or mini-circle and members operate according to the rules and expectations associated with this structure. The nature of their communication in both pyramids and circles will either create or destroy the connections that are the essence of an effective group.

Agreeing on the Rules

The effectiveness of the group depends upon the connections that group members develop among themselves; the strength of these connections rests upon the degree to which members have acknowledged a set of shared rules or expectations common to all group members. When these rules and expectations mesh with the stated purposes of a group, they form the basis for productive and satisfying interaction. Group members know basically what to expect from each other. When this basic cohesion is present, unexpected behavior on the part of some individuals may enliven group interaction without destroying it. However, when group members do not know what to expect from each other, and clear expectations do not draw members together around a common purpose, the group as currently constituted may dissolve in order to pursue other goals (see Figure 7.1).

The process of uncovering shared expectations - and agreeing, however tacitly, on the rules - involves the willingness of each group member to share personal expectations and to listen to those of others. As individuals share their own expectations with each other, they test and challenge each other. As they find that others share some of their own views of people and the world, they grow in acceptance of each other. This acceptance then is the foundation for effective group interaction. In an effective group, where interaction is based on a set of understood rules and expectations, there are no overwhelming surprises. All of the group's terrain is clearly defined, enabling individuals to circumvent pitfalls and to walk confidently in the open spaces.

Groups failing to uncover shared sets of expectations are subject to many hazards. Some group members, responding

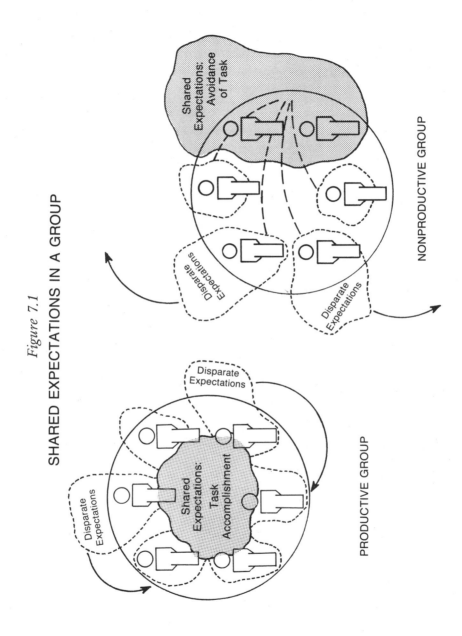

Figure 7.1

SHARED EXPECTATIONS IN A GROUP

warily to signs of unexpected disagreement, may choose to be quiet and withdraw. Others may plunge forward, determined to sweep away all potential disagreements. Still others, unaware that their peers may think differently from themselves, blithely express their own opinions and then are shocked and dismayed at the ensuing unexpected conflict. When individuals in groups operate without a common foundation much is left to chance, resulting in generally lowered productivity and satisfaction.

Effective Communication

Creating a shared set of expectations requires that group members tell others what they honestly think and listen receptively to others' views. Telling others what one thinks is termed *directness* in communication. Listening to what others think is termed *responsiveness*. Communication that is both direct and responsive is effective. Through effective communication, group members forge lasting links with each other.

Very Direct and Very Responsive

The importance of directness and responsiveness in communication cannot be overstated. We have watched individuals interacting in various groups, and have concluded that individuals who are both very direct and responsive are the ones to assume the roles of informal leadership within any group. As they state their own views, and listen to those of others, they guide the group in problem solving and decision making. The outcome of group process will clearly reflect the activities of the best communicators within that group setting. We have come to call these individuals *centers of influence* who are high in *change capability*. Not only do such people achieve their own goals, they help others to achieve theirs.

Further, such individuals within groups who are both direct and responsive tend to develop these qualities in others. Over a period of time they do not stand head and shoulders above others, but instead shoulder to shoulder with their peers. Such individuals, by not only stating *their* position but encouraging others to share theirs, elicit strength and develop talents in others. Consequently, over time, effective groups contain members who are direct and responsive, who are able to share their views and encourage others to do the same. The process of developing such an effective group, however, may begin with only one person who is strong in both directness and responsiveness.

Two examples of individuals using direct and responsive communication are Susan Tetweiler and Kenneth Bachman. Ms. Tetweiler is a 55-year-old manager in a large service organization. She is highly regarded by those who work with her; as one co-worker said, "everybody just loves Susan." Her behavior in a committee meeting in which she won her point demonstrates why people both respect and love her. She was very clear about her own needs but also very warm and receptive to the ideas of others.

She began her presentation by looking around at the other members and saying, "I need your help." She went on to explain how she had no place to meet with her clients since another manager was using the only spare room in the building to store old equipment. She had asked him to move and he had removed materials from one shelf so that she would have a place for *her* materials, but he had not vacated the room. Committee members asked numerous questions about the allocation of space and the priority of various sorts of needs within the company. It looked for a minute as if Ms. Tetweiler might get swept away by their questions and give up her point. However, she sat up straighter, put her feet squarely on the floor, looked them all in the eye in turn, and said, "But you have to understand, I *want* that room." Immediately, the entire committee relaxed and laughed and said they would act to get it for her. The meeting concluded when one man joked, "Let's just simplify the process and put out a contract on him." They all left laughing and Ms. Tetweiler now has her desired space.

Kenneth Bachman is a 52-year-old manager in a major corporation. In a series of task force meetings, he demonstrated his ability to bring a group to consensus without forcefully taking the lead in the discussion. In early meetings of the task force, a conflict had developed between two other members: Bill Allerton, a forceful young man, designated as a brilliant comer in the organization, and Cal Dudley, a slightly older man who had a reputation for getting things done in the traditional manner. At the beginning of the task force meetings, Mr. Allerton and Mr. Dudley had locked horns on several issues. Mr. Allerton would present his point; Mr. Dudley would challenge it. Mr. Allerton would press his point, and Mr. Dudley would become angry. The first meeting ended with Mr. Allerton pounding the table, and Mr. Dudley sitting back in the chair scowling with his arms crossed and his eyes looking at the papers on the table.

During this initial session, Mr. Bachman occasionally made a point but spent most of the time watching and listening to the two other men. In later sessions, however, he moved his chair in closer and took a greater part in the discussion. He would often lean forward and state an opinion (his way of looking at it) that encompassed the points of view of both men. Each would pause and agree with him, and then - in surprise - realize that they were agreeing with each other. Mr. Bachman continued this practice, interjecting when necessary, making statements that in fact showed that the points of view being expressed at the table were not contradictory but compatible. Soon, when he said, "Well, let's look at it this way..." he had everyone's full attention. Mr. Bachman's easy manner, his ability to get across to the others, and his insightful assessment of the situation established an atmosphere in which everyone got down to work. At the completion of their project, the task force was selected by the president of the company for special commendation.

Very Direct and Unresponsive

Many of our stereotypes of aggressive businessmen portray individuals who are very direct and unresponsive. The stereotypes also suggest that these individuals are highly successful within organizations. Our experience however has shown that this is not so. Rather, individuals who are aggressive (direct and unresponsive) are often highly visible within groups and within larger organizational units but they carry very little influence in problem-solving and decision-making. Such individuals are sometimes best characterized as *noisemakers*, rather like fireworks on the Fourth of July - except that their explosions are greeted with rather less satisfaction than genuine fireworks displays. Two groups whose meetings were characterized more by directness than responsiveness are described below.

The first example is a meeting among supervisors in a manufacturing plant. In this session, three of the supervisors present were very strong in presenting their opinions but demonstrated little responsiveness to others. As a consequence, these three frequently interrupted each other and other group members; one scowled and threw up his hands whenever another spoke, and another rarely spoke without pointing a pencil or a finger at the other members of the group. There was little consensus at the table, and the one who spoke loudest carried the day. All group members left the meeting disgruntled, feeling that they had been done in.

The second example is drawn from a series of continuous group meetings that occurred once a week for ten weeks. The group was composed of three women and two men. One of the women initially dominated the group, in part because of her extensive experience in administrative positions. In the first sessions, others listened to this woman's opinions with some interest. As the group moved into the fourth and fifth session, however, there was increasing restlessness among most group members and traces of hostility toward this woman, who continued to dominate the group. Anyone watching the sixth session would have seen the group fall into what had become a typical stance. The dominant woman continued to talk. Many of the group members pulled their chairs farther and farther away from her. Almost all of them eventually leaned back with their arms crossed. Several were frowning. Others were tapping pencils. They had clearly closed themselves off to her influence.

Very Responsive and Indirect

Contrary to the stereotypes noted, we have found that many groups of businessmen tend to be more responsive than direct. Particularly in corporate settings that discourage the expression of individual opinions, many employees have developed a communication pattern that is very attentive to others but that masks their real thoughts and feelings. Occasionally such individuals will allow another to lead for them and they, as a consequence, lower their level of commitment to any outcome of the decision-making processes. Other times all individuals in a group will operate in this manner, giving everyone the impression that they are operating in limbo, with no firm guidelines or expectations.

In contrast to the noisemakers, individuals who are very responsive and indirect are often *saboteurs,* and their point of view may not be known for a time. Only when a group is supposed to act on a common project is their opinion apparent, more often by what they do not do than what they do. In the face of action, they may demonstrate passive resistance because the agreed-upon plan did not include their own ideas (which were left unstated). Two descriptions of groups characterized by responsiveness without directness follow.

In the first instance, the manager of one manufacturing unit was rated highly by his employees on listening. However, the evaluations in other areas were only moderate - and occasionally weak. His employees complained that he did not set clear expectations for them and that they did not know what he wanted them to do. He would listen... and listen... but did not tell his employees *what he thought* and consequently they often felt that they were walking around as if in a swamp, without firm footing.

A second instance is drawn from a group meeting of another unit. In this case all members demonstrated very responsive behavior - except one. This one person talked and everybody else indicated their willingness to listen by leaning across the table, by nodding in response, and by focusing on the one person who spoke most of the time. As this person arrived at a decision, everybody else nodded in agreement. However, when the group dispersed, none of the "responsive" members of the group put aside any time or energy to carry out the decision; they did not feel it was *their* decision but rather *his* - the property of the one person who spoke up during the meeting.

In summary, effective communication is both very direct and very responsive. Individuals who are direct and *not* responsive may generate a lot of noise and create irritation among their colleagues, but generally carry less weight in decision-making processes than many other individuals. On the other hand, people who are responsive and *not* direct may sabotage group activity because their point of view seldom surfaces until the time for action is past, and they will resist accomplishing goals to which they have not agreed. Those people, however, who are both direct and responsive generally become informal leaders in groups and, over time, encourage the development of similar qualities in other group members. The directness and responsiveness of most group members then establishes a base of shared expectations from which effective groups can operate.

Pyramids and Circles

As group members interact, their shared expectations reflect a common understanding of the purposes of the group. Some groups are brought together primarily to accomplish tasks. Other groups meet primarily to share information. As the expectations of the group focus on a particular purpose, effective groups will assume the particular shape or structure that is appropriate to their purpose. Thus, some groups will become more pyramidal, in order to achieve specific objectives, and some groups will become more circular, in order to share information. The structure that the group adopts will arise from the understanding of the purposes of the group. The structure is, therefore, a function of shared group expectations. However, the structure also will influence those expectations - and the communication that occurs.

Communication in Pyramids

Pyramids are designed to get things done and have a hierarchical structure; in this setting communication is appropriate when it facilitates accomplishing tasks and occurs within a context where various levels of authority are respected and honored. Relevant information is always related to accomplishing goals, implementing procedures and evaluating performance (see Figure 7.2).

Communication in Circles

Circles are designed to share information, and have an egalitarian structure. Expectations about communication are consonant with those characteristics. Communication is

Figure 7.2

COMMUNICATION IN PYRAMIDS AND CIRCLES

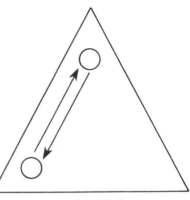

Sender-Receiver Unequal in
Status and Function

Task-Centered and Channeled

Communicating Information
for Task Accomplishment,
Implementing Procedures,
and Evaluating Performance

PYRAMIDS

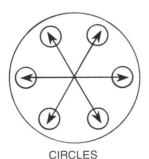

Sender-Receiver Equal
in Status & Function

Personal and Open

Clarify Problems and
Generate Alternatives

CIRCLES

appropriate when people are personal and open with each other and speak along a multiplicity of channels, sharing not only facts, information, and ideas but personal experience as well. Information that is communicated in circles is accepted as relevant whatever the nature, for within circles people welcome the experience of others however idiosyncratic. A variety of viewpoints enhances the group's interaction, resulting in the generation of as many new ideas and approaches as possible to any particular problem at hand while enlarging the experience of each individual member (see Figure 7.2).

Communication and Effective Structures

As long as communication - in either pyramids or circles - is both direct and responsive, group members will share their own expectations and listen to those of others. They will have a shared understanding of the purposes of the group, and as purposes shift, the group will take a new shape that is appropriate for new purposes.

Groups that resist information from both within and without never develop the ability to clarify new functions and purposes as they emerge, as a result of circumstances both within the group and in the outer environment. Such groups become structures of the past, unable to deal with a changing present. Communication is, therefore, the process through which groups maintain their ability to live in and adapt to a changing environment. Communication, in short, maintains the flexibility of any structural formation and allows the structure to adapt to changing circumstances.

Rules of Up-Down Communication in Pyramids

In the past decade we have focused as a culture on improving circular communication, in other words giving equal weight to the potential contributions of all members. We have at least been exposed to a set of rules for good circular communication. We have emphasized the importance of sharing our own experience and of listening to others share theirs. Americans on the whole have focused on the importance of relationships. Many of us have learned how to talk to others within a circular environment. As organizations once again become the focus of our cultural attention, however, it becomes clear that we don't always know how to talk to one another when we do not occupy equal positions. With new emphasis on participative management, bosses are being asked to share information with their employees on a more continual basis. Employees are also being asked to share their ideas, suggestions, and opinions with their bosses. We are slowly acknowledging that we need to talk with each other, but the labels of hierarchy hang over the doors of communication. We do not know the rules for communication in pyramids.

Communication Up and Down

In pyramids, rules or expectations about communication are related to an individual's place within a hierarchy. Rules for those above differ from those below. Although each individual may be above and below someone else, different rules will govern his or her behavior, depending on the status relationship within which the communication occurs. Effective communication occurs when individuals, whether above or below, have taken the time to respond to the other's position as well as their own.

From Bottom to Top

Those on the lower rungs of the organizational ladder are often inhibited from communicating upward for fear of negative evaluations. Often, however, their communication is welcomed - when it is expressed in line with the expectations of those above them. In general, there are several specific rules governing upward communication. Following these rules increases the probability that individuals will be heard (see Figure 7.3).

Figure 7.3

APPROPRIATE COMMUNICATION IN PYRAMIDS

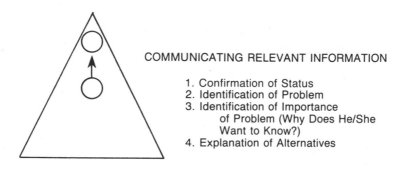

COMMUNICATING RELEVANT INFORMATION

1. Confirmation of Status
2. Identification of Problem
3. Identification of Importance
    of Problem (Why Does He/She
    Want to Know?)
4. Explanation of Alternatives

COMMUNICATING RELEVANT INFORMATION

1. Confirmation of Value to
    Operation
2. Explanation of Decisions
    and Rationale
3. Presentation of All Necessary
    Information Related to Topic
4. Clarity on Procedures and
    Expected Results

Confirming Status. Speakers fare better when they recognize and confirm the superior status of the other person. Doing so removes fears that the subordinate may be implying, "I can do your job better than you can." Status may be confirmed by both verbal and non-verbal behaviors. Verbal signals include, "Are you busy?" (indicating an awareness of the superior's time constraints); "I appreciated hearing your advice the other day" (indicating an awareness of the value of their ideas); "I know you have the final say" (recognizing their authority); and many others. Nonverbal signals include not intruding on a superior's space without invitation, not gesturing in demanding or evaluative ways, not staring or backing the other down.

Clarifying Relevance. Those speaking to superiors are responsible for making sure that their communication is relevant to the other. Often, the immediate concerns of those lower down are of little interest to superiors. In general, the most welcome information is relevant to getting things done. Such information may be important to achieving organizational goals. Much information may indeed fill the bill on this issue, but the speaker has another responsibility. Without wandering, digressing, and moving into personal experiences and emotional accounts, the speaker is responsible for presenting the information in such a way that the relevance to the superior is clear and evident. Sometimes those lower down enter the offices of those higher up with concerns that are relevant to the organizational goals, but expect the superior to make the connections himself or herself. This leaves the reception of such communication in the hands of the other. By shaping the communication so that relevance to task accomplishment is apparent, the speaker enhances his or her probability of being heard and understood.

Relating to Organizational Objectives. The speaker is responsible as well for elucidating the importance of the information in terms of organizational objectives. Why does it matter that this point be heard? What difference does it make? What will be the outcome? Is the outcome of measurable import compared to other matters which are pending? Those lower in the organization can be sure that their voice will be listened to when they have important matters to discuss. But the phrasing of the matter, and the justification, lies in the hands of the speaker.

Presenting Alternative Solutions. In presenting a possible solution to a problem, the speaker may also propose alternatives to this potential solution. Each potential solution ought to be backed by logical argument about possible consequences. As each solution is presented, however, the direction of conversation depends on the person of higher status. What the decision will be is in his or her purview, and not in that of the subordinate. Thus, having presented a good case, the subordinate may relax, for it is most likely that his or her point of view has been received.

From Top to Bottom

Other rules govern the behavior of superiors who wish to win the acceptance, and engage the motivation, of their subordinates.

Confirming Personal Value. Superiors are more receptively heard by their subordinates when they recognize and confirm the value of each person. The superior may indeed be higher in company status but not in human worth. Consequently, when the superior acknowledges the subordinate as a person of merit, it more likely that each will hear the other. Again, this information may be conveyed by verbal and nonverbal signals. Phrases such as "I'm glad to see you again," "I hear you've been doing good work," "Your opinion has always been helpful," indicate the receptiveness of the superior to the subordinate. Also, nonverbal behaviors such as moving away from a desk, minimizing evaluative gestures, maintaining eye contact, and nodding in response to the other's speech all indicate a receptivity to, and a recognition of the value of, the other person.

Explaining Decisions. A high-status person recognizes subordinates as valued members of the work team by explaining decisions to them and providing rationales for behavior. Recognizing that the desire to know about what is going on is universal and not one reserved for high status individuals validates the other person.

Presenting Sufficient Information. Explanations are enhanced by the presentation of all material relevant to the issue. Presenting sufficient information allows others the opportunity to evaluate and examine decisions as well as to confirm them. In presenting enough information for another to come to his or her conclusions, the high-status person says that the subordinate's thoughts and opinions matter.

Clarifying Expectations. Communication is improved when superiors are clear with their expectations of others' performance, when they identify procedures, and when they outline expected results. Subordinates do not then run the risk of doing what they think they are supposed to - only to discover that it is, in fact, contrary to expectations. Clarifying expectations gives subordinates the chance to think about them, and to choose whether or not to meet them. When expectations are not clear, subordinates grop in the dark, with only luck to fall back on in terms of succeeding at a given task.

Communication and Group Effectiveness

Effective communication and productive work is based on individuals' ability to both express their own expectations and to be open to the expectations of others. (Another way of saying this is that individuals need to agree to the same set of unspoken rules). When expectations coalesce around a group purpose, the foundation is laid for effective group functioning. Whether in pyramidal or circular structures, the purposes of the group will be met most effectively by individuals who are direct and responsive in communication. Within pyramids, direct and responsive individuals will acknowledge the status of others in the group. Within circles, such individuals will facilitate the open sharing of information among equals. Direct and responsive individuals become centers of influence within the group and cause others in the group to increase their own degrees of influence as well. A group containing many such individuals becomes the focus of change within the organization.

EXERCISE: SAYING WHAT YOU WANT TO SAY

Find one other person with whom to do this exercise. Each of you review the following questions and decide how you would respond to them. When you are ready, share your answers with your partner. Allow one person to speak first. The listener may ask clarifying questions but may not interrupt or evaluate what is being said. When this person is finished speaking, switch roles letting the other person speak as the first one responds.

1. What are the qualities (talents, skills, personality, characteristics) required for success in your current position? Are there areas in which you would like to learn new patterns of behavior? Do you have particular talents for which you would like more recognition?

2. What would you like to see change in your work environment in the next two years? five years? Do you think it is possible for these changes to occur? What can you do to see that they happen?

3. Imagine that you were going to retire in the next ten years. At this imaginary retirement party, your employees write a speech about you that describes their real opinion of you. What do you think they would say? What would you like them to say? Is there a difference? What can you do to be the kind of supervisor you would like to be?

When you have finished speaking, evaluate your own communication and that of your partner according to a simplified version of the **Personal Presentation Inventory** used to evaluate nonverbal behavior.

MINI-PERSONAL PRESENTATION INVENTORY

Place a number from 0 to 3 in each space (0 is low, 3 is high), indicating the degree to which you think you and your partner demonstrated the following behaviors:

	Self	**Partner**
Spoke clearly	_____	_____
Looked other in the eye	_____	_____
Faced other directly	_____	_____
Sat in a relaxed manner	_____	_____
Gestured for emphasis	_____	_____
Spoke with expression	_____	_____
Leaned forward	_____	_____
Nodded in response	_____	_____
Smiled	_____	_____
Total (+)	_____	_____
Mumbled	_____	_____
Looked away	_____	_____
Turned away	_____	_____
Crossed arms	_____	_____
Tapped, jiggled, or twitched	_____	_____
Yelled or spoke in monotone	_____	_____
Leaned back	_____	_____
Pointed fingers or pencils	_____	_____
Scowled, frowned or grimaced	_____	_____
Total (-)	_____	_____

Change Capability = Total (+)
                     - Total (-) = _____   _____

If your score is between 18 and 27, you demonstrate **high** change capability and are probable a **center of influence** in your environment.

If your score is between 9 and 18 you demonstrate **moderate** change capability and are only occasionally a **center of influence** in your environment.

If you score is below 9, you demonstrate **low** change capability and are only rarely a **center of influence** in your environment.

(For further information on the interpretation of your scores see **Organizational Sync.**)

Eight
On Knowing the Unspoken
Group Rules

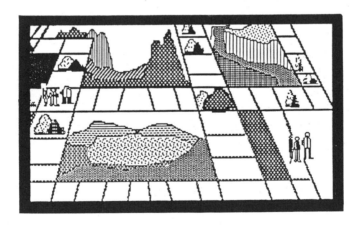

Travelers learned the different ways of the other players in the hills and the valleys - if they did not learn the ways that governed behavior in the settings through which they passed their journey might be made much more uncomfortable. In order to insure their physical and emotional safety, they watched and listened and were willing to learn of the ways of others.

The travelers knew there were many ways of working and living but many of the other players did not know this, thinking that their particular way was the way of the world . . . and because it was so it could not be changed.

The strongest influence on organizational behavior may well be the unspoken group rules created by each unit, division or organization. In one division of a manufacturing facility, for example, supervisors "zing" each other, yelling put-downs back and forth across the roar of the machinery. In another division supervisors refrain from what they perceive as rowdiness and keep their conversations focused on the task. In still another division individuals may laugh and joke but only quietly, for raising one's voice is considered to be in poor taste. Yet none of the workers in these situations are aware of any specific rule governing their behavior, nor are they conscious that their own behavior may change as they move from one setting to the next or as they work with different groups of individuals. Only someone coming into a new division, or taking a comparative survey, recognizes the differences between groups.

A supervisor transferring from the quiet division to the noisy one is appalled at the roughness of the men and does not perceive the camaraderie that lies behind the put-downs. A supervisor transferring from the noisy division into the restrained, task-oriented one is equally appalled at what he perceives as the unfriendly attitude of the other workers. In each setting, without really being aware of it, workers have adopted a set of rules governing their behavior. These sets of rules or expectations, sometimes called group norms, exert a powerful influence on individual behavior. If individuals and organizations are going to change, group norms are also going to have to change.

Learning the Rules

The rules which govern peoples' behavior in groups have been defined in a variety of ways. They may be made explicit in regulations, or procedures. Or, as is more often the case, these rules are implicit and not verbalized, with organizational members not even aware of their existence or of the ways in which they shape individual behavior. Existing on the implicit level, these rules about group behavior have been referred to as customs or traditions. Although events may be interpreted in terms of these rules, *why* they are interpreted this way is often not understood; people tend not to believe that these roles arose from a specific incident in history but rather that "this is the way things are." Alfred Schutz, a German sociologist, has described the operation of these rules - group norms - as "thinking-as-usual," a way of being and operating that is seldom questioned.

These group norms originate with the expectations of the

initial members of any group, and eventually come to be accepted over time as an implicit set of assumptions, a "thinking-as-usual" by which the group conducts its business. Those most influential in the group - that is, who are most direct and responsive - carry the greatest weight in terms of shaping the original norms or rules. Then the group itself develops a history imbued with these norms. As new members enter the group their expectations also have an impact on strengthening or redirecting existing group norms, depending on the strength of their own directness and responsiveness (see Figure 8.1).

Group rules or expectations include beliefs about how people should act in certain situations and, as such, have a strong impact on individual behavior. Groups that have been successful in meeting their own expectations - and in accomplishing their stated goals - are often tolerant about the behavior of their members. Such groups may tolerate more deviance among group members. On the other hand, groups that have been unsuccessful in attaining goals tend to tighten their control over individual behavior, as if the increased cohesiveness and apparent similarity of group members may compensate for lack of success in other ways.

Group Climate

The rules by which groups conduct themselves also shape the climate of the organization. Many groups, operating together, determine the atmosphere of the organization and, to a large extent, influence the productivity and satisfaction of all individuals in the workplace. Climate has been defined above as the set of shared perceptions or expectations of individual members of an organization. Climate can also be defined as

Figure 8.1

GROUP EXPECTATIONS AND
THE ORGANIZATIONAL CONTEXT

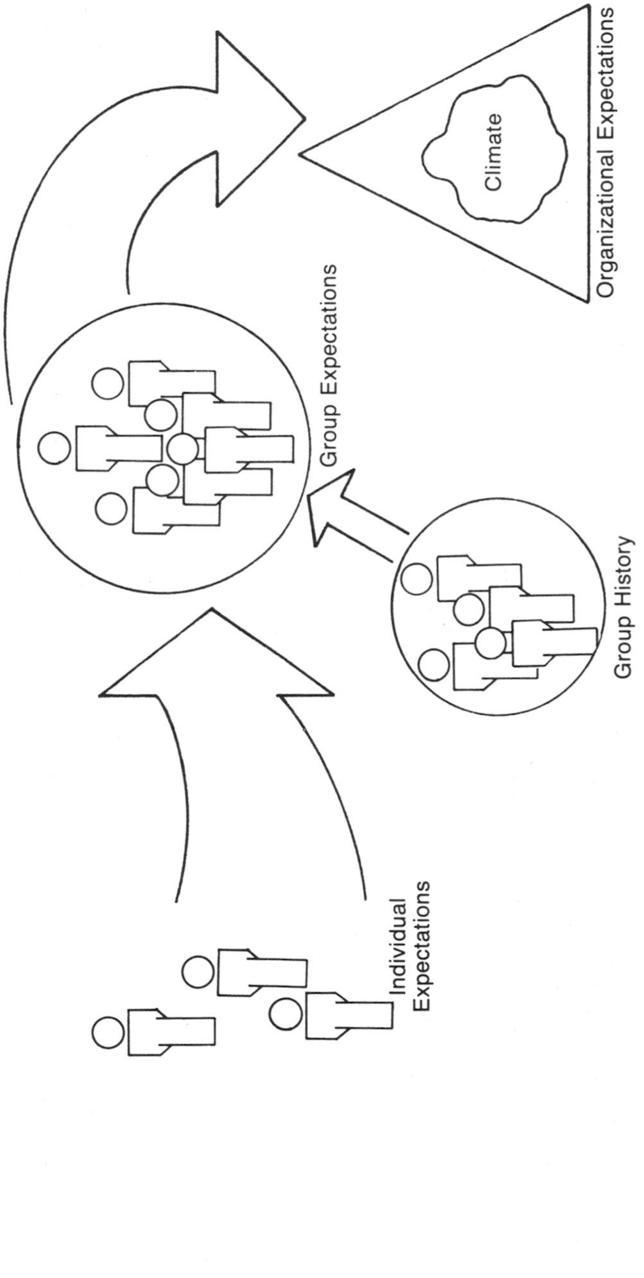

Individual Expectations

Group History

Group Expectations

Climate

Organizational Expectations

the shared perceptions or expectations of different groups within the organization, the group being the intermediary between the individual and the total system. Thus, group expectations affect not only the individuals in the group, but also the tone or atmosphere of the total organization, providing the framework for the system's informal operations.

The climate of an organization is permeated with the implicit expectations of that organization. The climate, in effect, is the unseen force establishing standards of conduct, encouraging individuals to respond negatively to what is seen as deviant behavior, and encouraging individuals to reward behavior that is in accord with implicit expectations. The shared perceptions and expectations within an organization thus regulate patterns of behavior, so that members with unacceptable behavior are disciplined and those with acceptable behavior rewarded. Thus over time, behavior within organizations becomes predictable as people interact with one another according to patterns established by group norms.

The climate also acts as a filter that allows certain information in and keeps other information out. Data that is not congruent with implicit expectations may be rejected, distorted, or not heard. Data that is in accord with the beliefs of group members will be circulated (see Figure 8.2). The degree to which the organization is effective in maintaining a set of unwritten rules will, to some extent, determine the cohesiveness of groups within the organization. The effectiveness of the these groups, however, will depend not only on acceptance of group norms, but on the constructive or destructive nature of these norms with respect to organizational purposes.

Figure 8.2
CLIMATE EFFECTS

NORMS
TRADITIONS
RULES
CUSTOMS

Effect on Individual
1) Control
2) Discipline
3) Patterns for Behavior

Effect on Group
1) Regularize Patterns
   for Individual and Group
2) Determine Cohesiveness
3) Filter Information

Constructive and Destructive Rules

Group rules that encourage the accomplishment of tasks and the sharing of information may be regarded as constructive within an organizational context. Within pyramidal structures, those unspoken group rules focusing on accomplishment will be more important; within circular structures, rules that encourage the dissemination of information will be more critical to group effectiveness. In either structure, however, both kinds of expectations are essential to effective group functioning.

Constructive group rules - in either setting - focus on the *purpose* of the group. Destructive group rules focus on the *appearance* of the group. In pyramidal group settings, constructive group rules will reward those who accomplish tasks and discipline those who do not. In contrast, destructive group rules will reward those who appear to be getting things done because they have higher status or more control over others. In circular group settings, constructive group rules will reward those who share openly with the group and are responsive to others. On the other hand, destructive group rules will reward those who appear to be sharing with others only because they spend more time in the group setting or because they never say anything with which someone might disagree. In short, constructive group rules require that members focus on the task at hand, whereas destructive group rules aid members in avoiding confrontation with the immediate tasks and purposes that further organizational goals.

Group Rules and the Process of Change

In order for individuals and organizations to change, the unspoken rules that govern the behavior of individuals must also change. Individuals who change their behavior in ways that contradict group rules or expectations usually call down upon themselves the disapproval of the group; their new behavior is regarded as strange or unusual, and usually leads to a bad end. In order for new individual behavior to be accepted, group rules must change to tolerate such new behavior. In like manner, organizational edicts about changes in procedures, policies, and style will run into considerable interference when tacit group rules are not in accord with the new ways of being. Unless these rules change, groups pay only lip service to new organizational goals, and individual members do likewise, subverting any efforts to implement new procedures.

Therefore, any effort at organizational change requires that the underlying assumptions of the organization, and of its composite groups, be analyzed and brought into awareness. This is not a simple process, since patterns of behavior that have been unquestioned and that are believed to be "simply the way things are" are not easily recognized or challenged. The process of changing group expectations proceeds slowly and over many stages, as individuals within organizations come first to recognize, then to accept, and finally to change those group norms not compatible with current individual and organizational goals.

Recognizing the Rules

Several questions may be asked to uncover the group rules governing behavior in any group. The questions are: *What* is happening in the group? *How* is it happening? *Why* is it happening? Focusing on each of these questions in turn can lead to a greater awareness of underlying group rules, and of the effects that they have on guiding individual behavior in groups.

What is Happening?

Individuals often do not see what is actually happening around them; rather, they see what they expect to see. If, however, they are asked to focus on actual behavior and to describe that behavior specifically, they are likely to be able to put aside their expectations to observe what is actually transpiring in their environment. As individuals make efforts to note specific behaviors, and to chronicle events without interpretation, they begin to describe the patterns of behavior that actually occur in their group. They increase their skill in observation and listening, sensitizing themselves to behaviors and more subtle cues that indicate the direction of events in their group. For example, in observing communication processes within a group, individuals may note which parties talk most, to whom, and in what order. Their observations will be a record of *what* is happening in the communication (see Figure 8.3).

Figure 8.3

IDENTIFYING GROUP NORMS I

What Is Happening?

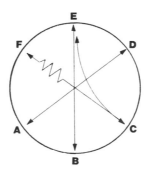

Who talks most?
Who supports whom?
Who interrupts whom?

How is it Happening?

Observation of how people communicate with each other adds further information about group interaction. *How* do people make contacts with each other? *How* do they speak to each other? Does their tone indicate openness, rejection, restraint, aggression, warmth, or anger? With some minimal interpretation, individuals learn from noting the actual language patterns, the verbal and nonverbal behavior, and the tone of what is occurring *how* individuals communicate. Each communication pattern may be interpreted within the framework of effective and ineffective pyramids and circles (see Figure 8.4).

Figure 8.4

IDENTIFYING GROUP NORMS II

How Is It Happening?

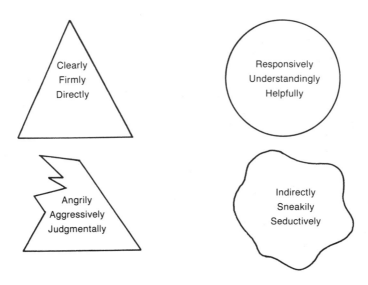

Why is it Happening?

It is in answering this question that further interpretation is required. As observers of human behavior, we may see *what* happens around us. With a little interpretation, we may describe *how* it happens. Then, from our knowledge of ourselves and others, we may form hypotheses about *why* people behave as they do. While we cannot see why things happen, we may make certain assumptions about causality. If we assume that there are logical explanations for most behavior, we can postulate the reasons why a given pattern of behavior is occurring. When we can minimize individual perceptual

Figure 8.5

IDENTIFYING GROUP NORMS III

Why Is It Happening?

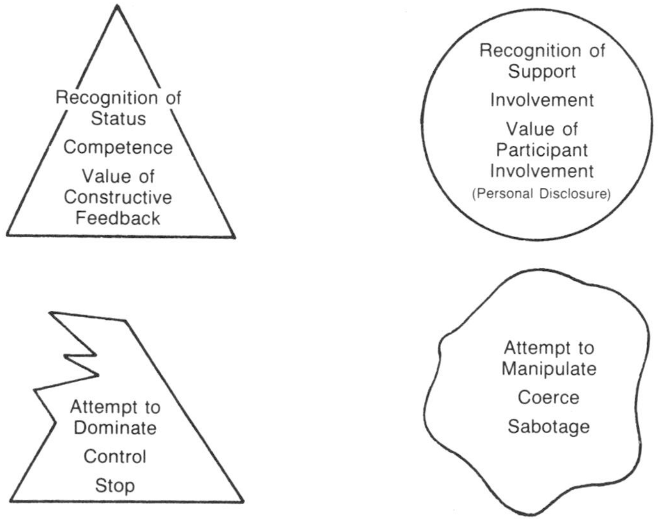

Recognition of Status
Competence
Value of Constructive Feedback

Recognition of Support
Involvement
Value of Participant Involvement
(Personal Disclosure)

Attempt to Dominate
Control
Stop

Attempt to Manipulate
Coerce
Sabotage

idiosyncrasies, our explanations can give us a clue as to the rules which govern behavior in both pyramids and circles (see Figure 8.5).

Evaluation of Old Rules and Implementation of New Ones

When individuals ask what, how, and why, they are able to identify old rules, and to decide whether or not to replace them with new ones. In the following example, an engineer asks "Why?" and discovers that a familiar expectation may be changed at considerable savings to the company.

"One man for each machine" was one of the unwritten rules in the production area of an industrial company. As the engineers in the company began to look at ways to cut costs, one of them questoned this rule. "Why," he asked, "can't one man run two machines?" "Because he can't see two machines at once," was the familiar and expected answer. The questioning engineer then suggested, that in several areas of the plant, machines that ran alternately with each other be turned around to face the same worker and be monitored as part of the same job. In each instance that this occurred, the company saved one person's salary without overtaxing the remaining worker.

In another example a group of people discover that their familiar expectations of each other, leading continually to friction between subgroups, can be changed by sharing information across subgroups.

Group expectations between two different functional areas in a manufacturing plant were such that each thought the other area was purposely slacking off and creating difficulty for the other. In a seminar meeting, supervisors at one table made a crack about the other group and the other group, at another table, responded. After initial barrages were fired at each other, two people, one from each group, decided to head off to the coffee room together. There they examined their assumptions about each other and countered faulty expectations with facts about their respective operations. When these two people returned, they asked both their tables to meet together and convinced the large group how little they knew about one another's operations - and the difficulties that each unit was facing. They arranged a meeting the upcoming week in which each group could share information, and eventually arrived at a scheduling procedure that could meet the needs of both units.

As individuals in groups learn to observe and then interpret their own behavior, they turn up information on which to base new - and more constructive - decisions. In each case, groups may *evaluate* group rules, *target* rules for change, and *implement* new rules.

Evaluation of Constructive and Destructive Group Rules

Once people identify why events occur as they do, or individuals behave as they do, they come close to identifying a group rule. They may then evaluate this rule by asking whether or not it helps the group to accomplish group or organizational goals. Does the rule facilitate task accomplishment or encourage individuals to share ideas with each other? Do group rules encourage development of innovative ideas and the implementation of effective procedures? Do they encourage openness to new information, clarification of problems, and a responsiveness to and trust in others?   One might ask alternately if the rules encourage malingering on the job, repress innovation, hamper the implementation process, limit communication, prevent analysis of problems, and encourage the development of fear as opposed to trust.

Some rules facilitate task accomplishment and are characteristic of effective pyramids.   Other group rules facilitate a smooth information flow and are characteristic of effective circles (see Figure 8.6).   Effective organizations as a whole include both effective pyramids and effective circles -- and organizational expectations supported by group norms that reward getting things done and create a sense of belonging among group members. The result of such sets of expectations is an organizational climate that furthers productivity and satisfaction.

Targeting Group Rules for Change

After group rules are evaluated, some of those that are counterproductive in terms of organizational goals may be targeted for change. For each targeted rule, the behavior (what), the process (how), and the rationale for that behavior (why) should be clarified. Strategies for change can then be selected that will reinforce a set of behaviors different from those previously reinforced. In the following example, supervisors choose to revise expectations about daily cleanup, and devise a new system of rewards for those who perform this function well.

A group of supervisors in a technical area of a manufacturing plant sat together for several hours examining the group rules shaping behavior in their unit. They quickly identified a

Figure 8.6

EVALUATING GROUP NORMS

DO GROUP NORMS:

1) Facilitate

Getting
Work
Done?

Innovation?

Implementing
Effective
Procedures?

Maximizing Output
from Limited Resources?

2) Facilitate

Openness to New
Information?

From Within?

From Without?

Clarification of Problems
and Alternatives?

Responsiveness to Others?

Trust and Support?

set of group rules that allowed their men to get away with "bad housekeeping." As a consequence, at the end of each of their shifts they were continually picking up for their men, putting equipment away, and getting the area ready for the next shift. The expectation of their men was that, regardless of their own behavior, their supervisors would cover for them by getting the unit clean for the incoming shift. The supervisors agreed to set up a new system in which they would put their energies not into picking up, but into monitoring cleanup crews among the men. They also devised a system of rewards to honor the crews that did the best job. Instituting the new group rules required a commitment of time and energy from all the supervisors. However, the early period of more intense effort on their part led, in the long term, to a more efficient and less taxing cleanup procedure.

In a different situation, another group of supervisors encouraged the development of responsibility among a larger group of workers by allowing more of them to participate in interesting tasks, seen as a reward in itself.

Within the production area of a manufacturing plant, several supervisors recognized they were perceived as playing favorites because they relied for assistance continually on subordinates whom they thought were the most responsible and capable. In thinking this through they realized that over the years they had developed one group of subordinates while neglecting to develop potential talent in other workers. Consequently they decided that each of them, in selecting individuals to assist in responsible positions, would select only two of three from the groups that had previously proven themselves, and would select one of three from the remainder of workers. Choosing a majority from the known group would insure satisfactory performance, and provide a check on the performance of the people given new responsibilities. Choosing one person from the rest of the groups would give other talent a chance to surface. In effect, without thinking much about it, they *had* played favorites by not offering opportunities to those who were newer in the organization. As they instituted their plan, the notion that they played favorites began to dissipate.

In each case, the group of supervisors instigating change made a clear commitment to focus time and energy during the initial period of transition implementing new behavior - aware that in the long run they, as well as their workers, would profit from the change in group expectations.

In another case, workers had a lot of difficulty analyzing group expectations within the organization. They backed up to focus on why it was so difficult for them to uncover shared expectations, or, in other words, why they did not perceive group rules in the same way. They discovered that the general emphasis on specialization had kept them isolated in different areas of the plant. Thus the basic unspoken rule targeted for change was an expectation of specialization, which blocked communication flow among workers in different areas. The specific situation which occurred is outlined below.

Several employees of a plant met with the goal of arriving together at some plans by which they could improve the functioning of their organization. As they talked about the expectations of their organization, they realized that each of them viewed these expectations from an entirely different perspective. One individual was a first-line supervisor who worked on the afternoon shift, and another worked in a specialty department on the day shift. Two other individuals were in higher-status positions in staff jobs - personnel and quality assurance.

As they experienced difficulty agreeing on the unspoken group rules governing their plant, they realized that one central expectation was at the root of their difficulty. Like many American industrial organizations, they were each adhering to a norm - a group rule - emphasizing the importance of speciali-zation of function. Because they were specialized, either in terms of shifts or functions, they were unable to perceive other expectations in the same light as their own. Once they realized this, they examined the group expectation that they remain in their separate functions, and found there was no overt regulation that said that they must do so.

The resultant plan was to view the organization from one another's perspective at least once by "walking in the other's shoes" for a day. Each member of this group was to take another's position for one day, and then the group would meet; from enhanced perspectives, they would then work on clarifying other unspoken rules of the organization.

Again, individuals examined what was occurring in their work setting, how it was occurring, and why it was occurring. They then identified group rules explaining *why* something was happening, and evaluated the constructive or destructive effect of these rules. Then they targeted the rule for change.

Implementing Strategies for Change

Finally, after individuals in a group target rules for change, they begin the process of implementing new group rules. Sometimes the implementation is a simple process, such as turning one of the machines around on the floor of a plant. Sometimes the process is more difficult, such as establishing new expectations for good housekeeping among a technical crew. Other times the rules may take years to implement, such as breaking down barriers that have arisen between functions, based upon expectations that specialization leads to effectiveness. Groups may begin this process, as in the examples above, by holding meetings, by changing roles, or by interchanging functions for a day. But spreading the process throughout a whole plant takes time. The process of change is usually rather slow, and the first step is the most difficult. Yet each of the groups described above took the first step and set in place the larger change process (See Figure 8.7).

Figure 8.7

CHANGING GROUP NORMS

1) IDENTIFY BEHAVIOR: What is done?
2) IDENTIFY PROCESS: How is it done?
3) IDENTIFY RATIONALE: Why is it done?

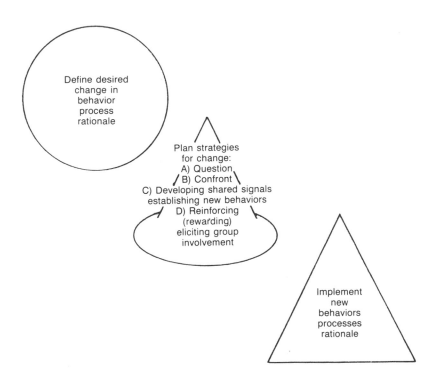

Group Rules and the Process of Change

Any change in individual or organizational behavior requires a change in the rules governing behavior within the group - and changes in the expectations of all the individuals collectively making up that group. When individuals want to change group rules, the process by which they enact change evolves through several steps. These steps may be summarized as follows:

1. Identify current behavior and events.
2. Identify process by which behavior and events occur.
3. Determine the most likely rationale for both the observed behaviors/events and the process by which they are carried out - in other words, identify rules.
4. Evaluate the rules in terms of their usefulness in facilitating task accomplishment or the sense of belonging to the group.
5. Create new rules to replace nonfunctional ones and develop the systems of feedback and reinforcement necessary to institute these changes.
6. Implement, over time, the new group rules, periodically evaluating progress toward this goal.

Any change in group rules will have effects beyond the immediate group involved, and will affect the organizational system in such a way as to provoke change in other groups as well.

EXERCISE:
GROUP RULES IN YOUR ORGANIZATION

A. Write down all the expectations for behavior (group rules or norms) that exist within your work group. If you have difficulty identifying them, spend some time observing people at work and ask What? How? and Why? about the events that you observe. Consider all areas of your work setting. Consideration of some of the following areas may help you further in identifying group norms.

Areas in which most groups have informal group rules:

Recognition of status	Openness to personal disclosure
Rewards for competence	Maintaining control and discipline
Value of constructive feedback	Displaying opposition
Means of feedback to each other	Allowing sabotage
Support for others	Coercing colleagues
Listening to others	Winning
Involving others in decisions	Losing

B. In the spaces below, identify the rules that facilitate task accomplishment and group maintenance (in effective pyramids and cirlces) and those that interfere with the pursuit of these goals (in ineffective pyramids and circles). Refer to the rules you have just listed.

	Effective	**Ineffective**
Pyramids	1. _____	1. _____
	2. _____	2. _____
	3. _____	3. _____
	4. _____	4. _____
	5. _____	5. _____

Circles 1. _____   1. _____

2. _____   2. _____

3. _____   3. _____

4. _____   4. _____

5. _____   5. _____

C. As a group, select one rule operational in your work setting that you will target for change. If a number of rules are interrelated and you desire to change all of them, they may all be listed. One rule, however, should receive highest priority.

1. Write down your rule selected for change. List other related rules.
2. Identify new rule(s) to be established in its (their) place.
3. What steps would you take to implement this change?
4. What would be the short- and long-term benefits of this change?

Nine
Managing the Change Process

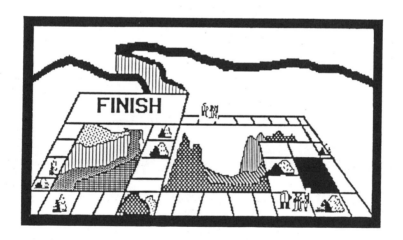

As the game continued, more and more players were swept from the board by the unwelcome power of the winds of change. The players of the hills and valleys who remained in the game spent much of their time in discomfort or fear: discomfort if their environment had been transformed or fear that such might soon be the case.

*With diminishing numbers of players, the fate of the entire gameboard was in jeopardy. Spurred by this realization, the travelers thought some more on the work skills of the hills and the thinking skills of the valleys, wondering why the those in the valleys did not **do** what they were imagining and those in the hills did not **think** beyond their immediate task. "What if," said one traveler to another one day, "the ideas of the valleys were linked with the achievements of the hills? Perhaps, the people themselves, thus joined together, might create **welcome** changes on the gameboard harnessing the power of the wind for the benefit of the players. . ."*

We can all think of times when we have tried to change something and failed. We had a good proposal and presented it to a supervisor, only to find it sitting on his desk for a week before finding its way to the trash can. Or maybe we worked hard at getting people in our unit to come to work on time only to discover some time later they were once again coming late - because the people in the next department were coming late. We have also sat in meetings where a boss (ourselves, perhaps) demanded that group members think of new ideas for some project, with dead silence the result; or we have also been in meetings where a good idea never got off the floor because nobody could decide who would do what; or if tasks were assigned, they were were never completed. Or we may have been part of a task force that needed only an hour or two more to complete a given project, when the group decided to meet at the nearest bar and to drink instead of to work (the project forgotten). All of these are common instances in which attempts at productive activity and change were, in some way, unsuccessful.

Every individual, however, has the capacity to successfully shape the process of change, the capacity to continually find new and effective ways of playing on the organizational gameboard. The phases through which one moves in this process are clearly identifiable. Further, in each phase certain difficulties are commonly encountered - and there are certain responses which then surmount these difficulties. Although, in reality, the phases may overlap with each other, or we may go through them more than once in a cyclic fashion, the purposes of each phase are best achieved when individuals adopt the appropriate structures, norms and behaviors. Any individual at work, any player on the gameboard, can manage a process of change by being willing to move through different structures, to do more than one thing at a time, and to accept, confront and overcome the difficulties always encountered in the change process.

The Time Line of Change

The change process can be placed along a time line (see Figure 9.1). The first stage is symbolized by a circle, since its primary purpose is to collect information, explore the nature of

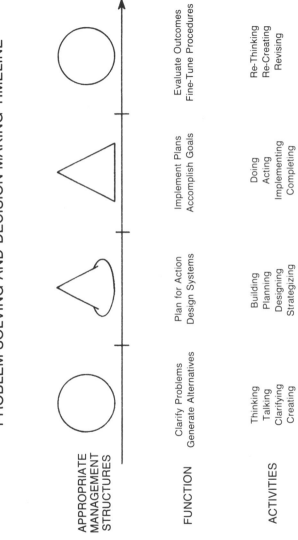

Figure 9.1

PROBLEM-SOLVING AND DECISION-MAKING TIMELINE

the problem, to clarify underlying assumptions about the problem, and to generate alternative solutions. The second stage is symbolized by a cone, for its purpose is to sift through ideas until an ultimate plan is selected. It requires both an openness to ideas and an ability to evaluate those ideas. The third stage is symbolized by a pyramid, for at this stage in the change process openness to ideas and information is less important than putting the plan into action; this stage is an implementation phase. As the process begins a new cycle, the pyramid yields to a circle as whatever has been done is examined and redesigned.

The Circular Phase

The initial phases of any change process benefit from as much information as possible. Suppose you want to change your own style of supervision. You go out and ask other people what is effective for them, you read books and articles, and perhaps take a class in management behavior. In fact, you collect as much information as possible about alternative patterns of behavior. The same holds true when individuals wish to change a group or an organization. It is necessary to gather as much information as possible so that one has examined the widest possible range of alternatives. At the beginning of the change process, casting as wide a net as possible to draw in relevant information is most important.

The best structure for this stage is the circle. A circle encourages communication and establishes expectations that all individuals are valuable and that their ideas are worthy of being heard. A circle may be envisioned as spread flat against the ground, having many points of contact with the environment.

The flatness of the structure allows information to move in all directions, and individuals within the structure can then use this information to clarify the nature of the problem. As the problem is examined from different sides, different forms of solutions emerge. Some of these alternative solutions follow past practices and standard procedures; others are more innovative in nature maybe even humorous or "off the wall." The initial period of any problem-solving or change process is designed to welcome and examine multiple inputs - before subjecting them to the screens and filters of the later phases (see Figure 9.2).

Figure 9.2

CIRCULAR PHASE

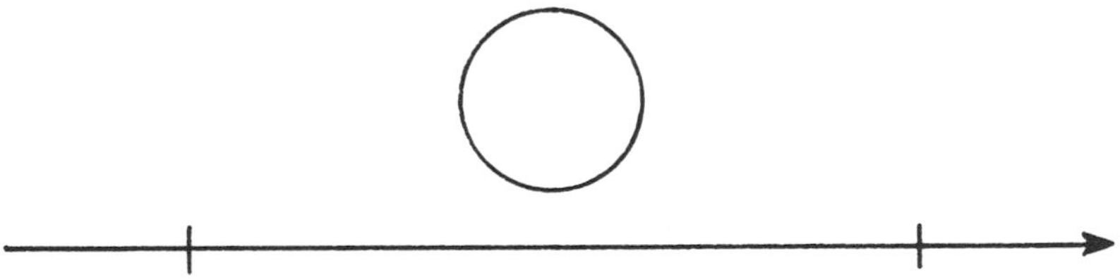

Clarify Problems
  Obtain information
  Identify patterns
  List contributing factors
Identify Goals
  Define specific outcomes
  Explore expected consequences
Generate Alternative Solutions

The Conical Phase

The screens and filters appear in the second phase, in which input is welcomed and then evaluated. Each suggestion is scrutinized to assess its possible outcomes and the possibilities for its implementation. The result of such scrutiny of the may different suggestions emerging from the circular phase is the development, finally, of a viable and significant plan of action. In many ways, this is the most important of all phases, because good planning minimizes error, and speeds implementation. There are three stages of this second phase (see Figure 9.3).

Prioritizing and Selecting an Alternative

By sifting through the information available from the circular phase, a definition of the problem must be agreed upon and alternative strategies identified. Two procedures are essential in this process: the first is to evaluate the possible outcomes of any alternative solution and to assess the *significance* of these outcomes; and the second is to test the *feasibility*, or the possibility of actual implementation, of the alternatives which may lead to a significant outcome.

Questions related to significance and feasibility may be seen as screens or filters through which one passes the information collected in the first phase - so that the selected alternative is both worthwhile and possible. To sift alternatives for significance the following questions are helpful: will the expected outcome make a positive difference for a number of individuals? how many units will be affected? what are the short-term effects? what are the long-term effects? how would implementation of this idea affect available resources, in the short- and long-term? Exploration of all possible outcomes of alternative solutions prevents any surprises from occurring in the later phase of implementation, and keeps energies focused on the goal throughout the planning stages.

Figure 9.3

CONICAL PHASE

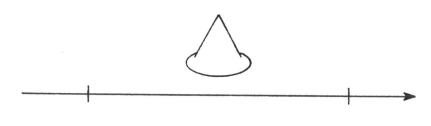

PRIORITIZING

      Select Problem and Alternative
        Determine significance
        Determine feasibility
      Re-evaluate Problem and Alternative

DELEGATION

      Develop Strategy
        Break out action steps
        Assign individual responsibility
        Elicit commitment

ACCOUNTABILITY

      Design Evaluation Measures
        Establish
        Create feedback channels
        Plan contingencies

To sift alternatives for feasibility requires asking a different set of questions: what are the resources necessary to carry out a given alternative? are such resources available or can they be obtained? how much time is involved? Many worthwhile projects die before they can begin because the resources for implementation are not at hand. Other times individuals give up change projects altogether because they do not believe that it is possible to implement them.

Actually, it is usually possible to implement at least part of a significant idea. Sometimes taking the first step is nearly as good as doing all of it - because the first step is the building block on which the rest can be built. Projects may fail because we want to do everything at once and do not plan instead for taking the small step which could be taken with available resources.

Delegating and Involving Others

Once an alternative is agreed upon, it is necessary to begin the process of involving others. All of those involved in various aspects of the plan need to either approve or or accept the idea in order for implementation to be successful. Questions about gaining approval and acceptance are of a different order from each other and consequently are addressed separately.

In order to obtain the necessary approvals for implementation of a new idea, the following questions are critical: what other people are going to be involved? have you created an idea that requires the approval of a multitude of individuals? if so, how could the idea be revised so that fewer people would have to approve? In the first example below, a group of supervisors failed to answer the last question successfully. In the second example, a group of women managers succeeded in choosing an alternative strategy in the face of similar problems.

In the first instance, some supervisors in a testing area faced what they regarded as a major problem. Because their "customers" from other areas of the company failed to fully complete the appropriate order forms for a variety of tests, tests were often delayed because necessary information was needed from individuals who were frequently difficult to find. The testing supervisors wanted to make their own operation more efficient by enforcing a policy of completely filling out the order forms. As they moved through the planning stages, however, they realized that enforcing such a plan would require approval of the 12 vice- presidents of the other units. Overcome with the impossibility of the task, they gave up altogether and resigned themselves to an ineffective situation.

In the second case, a group of women managers in a large communications company was trying to get a new type of performance appraisal adopted in the system. Faced with a personnel manager whose approval they thought (probably correctly) would not be forthcoming, they became very discouraged. Prodded by one of the women, however, they began to examine other alternatives. After a thorough examination of the personnel office they decided on one person, with considerable clout, who might be able to help them. They delegated two members of their group to approach this person the next day with a well-prepared plan and to ask for her help and advice.

Another set of questions highlights the importance of winning acceptance for the idea (in contrast to approval) from all of those who will be affected by the implementation of the idea: who will be affected? when will these individuals be informed of the idea? how will their acceptance be elicited? what procedures will be used to win their acceptance? Another example from another setting shows how one group failed to deal with these questions effectively.

A woman executive proposed a reorganization of her service unit. She calculated resources, talked with her superiors about the possibilities, and received their tentative approval before broaching it with immediate subordinates in her own unit. They suggested revisions for the plan but were basically enthusiastic about the proposal. As final signatures for implementation were being accepted, her boss casually mentioned the plan to four of her peers at a business luncheon. All of them quickly sat back in their chairs, scowled, and started voicing their objections. The woman executive was astonished. She hadn't thought their responses would be so intense nor their objections so vehement. She hadn't thought that they would be affected at all.

This example describes a situation in which the executive had answered all but one of the last questions which are critical to the second, conical phase of the planning process. In order to provide the best odds for success of a project all questions about resources, approval and acceptance must be satisfactorily answered. In other words, significance and feasibility must be thoroughly assessed. Then it is time to formally outline a strategy for achieving one's objectives.

Most of the answers to the following questions are readily available from a study of the significance and feasibility of an idea. Formally answering them in order, however, provides the outlines of the actual strategy which will be pursued in order to achieve a desired goal. The questions to be addressed are: what steps need to be accomplished in order to implement this plan? at what time must specific resources be acquired? at what time is it necessary to elicit the approval of key figures? when and how will you seek the acceptance of other individuals who will be at least peripherally affected by the implementation of this plan?

Responses to these questions outline the overall strategy for a proposed change project. Next specific steps must be outlined and placed along a time line. Individuals accountable for accomplishing each step must be noted. Time must be allotted not only for implementing the steps themselves, but for contacting all the individuals whose approval and acceptance are necessary. Finally, those most centrally involved in the planning process must commit themselves fully to the plan. Any objections or reservations should be brought to the surface, so that the concluding plan is strongly supported by all involved in its design.

Building in Accountability and Evaluation Procedures

The last part of the planning process involves designing the specific measures by which progress toward goal completion will be evaluated. The following questions address the issues of accountability and evaluation: how will progress be measured? by whom? when? how will information flow through the entire group so that all central figures are aware of the progress of this project? A breakdown in this process is illustrated in the following example.

In what was believed to be participative management style, the manufacturing unit of a major corporation "turned its people loose" by giving each of several units complete control of their production. When a central figure was asked "How is it going?" he replied, "How the hell do I know how it's going! Everybody's just doing their own thing!"

However, when plans for monitoring the process of implementation are included as part of the overall strategy, the chaotic result described above would be unlikely to happen. The conical planning stage then results in a time line of action steps, an allocation of responsibility to specific individuals and units, the design of feedback measures so that progress is noted, and the design of contingency measures to help sidestep obstacles when they occur. When all of these tasks are achieved, the conical planning phase is concluded.

The Pyramidal Phase

Ideas that pass successfully through the conical phase are likely to result in action plans ready for the next phase of the change process: successful implementation in the pyramidal phase (see Figure 9.4). This phase is characterized by accomplishing the tasks that have already been selected in the

Figure 9.4
PYRAMIDAL PHASE

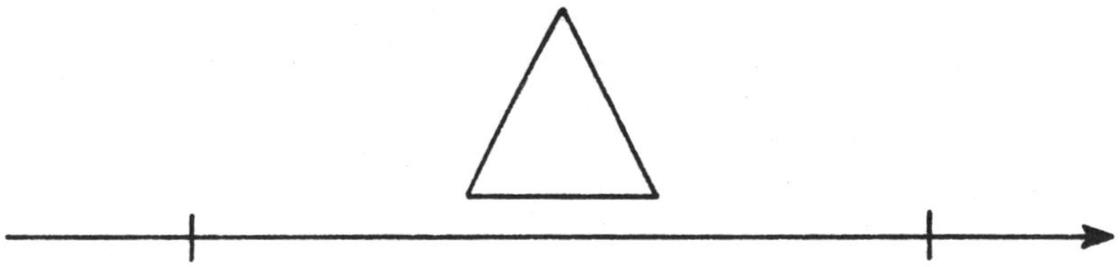

Implement Action Steps
Operationalize Feedback Channels
Identify Problem Spots
    Redesign action steps
    Implement contingencies
Monitor Progress
    Responsibility
    Accountability

conical phase. Once in this phase, groups become bogged down if they maintain wide-open information-gathering structures. Gathering information is no longer productive as the time for action has come.

When the planning stage has been thorough, the implementation stage proceeds quickly and without too many surprises. Feedback channels are operationalized, individual achievements are assessed and noted, and progress toward the objective is monitored. Contingency plans are activated if and when an obstacle is encountered.

Shaping the Change Process

In summary, the change process from beginning to end can be symbolized by a cyclical interaction between circles, cones, and pyramids within the organizational structure (see Figure 9.5). Circles begin the process and yield to cones; cones give way to pyramids; and pyramids eventually return again to circles. As each structure is suited to the function, circles, cones and pyramids appear and disappear. The flexibility of the structures is essential to effective monitoring of the change process. The following situation illustrates one attempt at implementing an idea through several levels of management.

In one plant of a major company with a strong participative philosophy, the following procedures were used when two of the larger sections of the plant were required to cut their costs by 15 percent. The two units' supervisory personnel met with their workers for several hours, explaining the situation to them and eliciting suggestions. Then the supervisors from each of the two units met in separate groups, and each developed an alternative strategy that fit with their own needs. Each supervisory

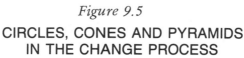

Figure 9.5

CIRCLES, CONES AND PYRAMIDS
IN THE CHANGE PROCESS

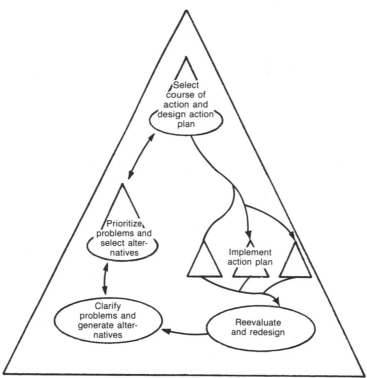

group estimated the changes in costs, productivity and employee morale that would result from the implementation of their strategy over a year's time. One member from each group then presented the particular unit's plan to top management. Members of the top management team then utilized the input from both groups in drawing up an overall strategy.

The following day upper management presented its own proposal to all of the individuals in the units involved. The two units met with one another to decide upon the degree to which they would "buy in" to management's plan. Recognizing that management had either incorporated the units' points of view or had taken the time to explain why various points had been rejected, the two units gave management a rather strong show of support. The upper management people, who had agreed beforehand to not go forward without support from the units, were pleased.

Tasks were then assigned which involved changing procedures, and increasing employee training and morale. Individual supervisors were made responsible for part of the larger program. Charts were mounted on walls to show weekly records of costs and productivity. All of the individuals involved knew where they were going and why - and that their jobs depended on causing the productivity chart to climb and the cost chart to fall. Collectively, they gave the effort their best shot. The change process is similar whether individuals are concerned with a specific personal problem, a difficult work relationship, or the shocks generated by environmental change. In any case, individuals have the option to either resign themselves to distressing situations - adapting themselves to restrictive circumstances - or to guide the process of change toward a constructive conclusion. What and how much individuals can do is very much contingent upon their particular situation, but individuals can always do *something*. And it's in doing something - creating a constructive plan and implementing it - that control of the change process returns to the hands of the individuals involved.

EXERCISE:
PROBLEM SOLVING AND THE CHANGE PROCESS

Read the story about the personal difficulties of Jim and Dave on the next pages. Use the following sheets to clarify alternatives for solving their interpersonal problem.

Each Man's An Idiot!

Jim and Dave both had the same position in two different divisions of a corporation. Both of them had the task of relaying reports between divisions and exchanging supplies and products on a regular schedule. Generally, they met together once a week to go over schedules and reports and to coordinate the efforts of the two divisions. For several years they had worked amicably together and people referred to them as a great team, since their work went without a hitch.

At the time our story takes place, however, it became clear to Jim's manager, Mark, that a change had taken place. Jim and Dave met only irregularly, schedules had been interrupted, and occasionally supplies had not been available for the production schedule. One man had commented to Mark that he'd seen Jim and Dave yelling at each other the day before. Mark said, "That's remarkable. Now that I think about it, I haven't noticed them speaking to each other at all."

A few days later, Bob, a friend of both Jim and Dave, asked if he could meet with Mark. When he came in, he apologized for taking his time, but said he was concerned about the relationship between Jim and Dave. A week ago, he had lunch with Jim to discuss the possibilities for a new routing system that he thought would increase efficiency. During their lunch Bob had mentioned Dave, asking Jim if Dave would be willing to cooperate. Jim burst out, "How the hell do I know what Dave wants? What an idiot! If you want to know what he thinks ask him!" Jim went on to express his anger at Dave.

Jim's story: "I don't know where Dave is anymore. He won't talk to me. Ever since he broke up with his wife, he's clammed up. When I suggest we do something, he says not to order him around and that he's tired of doing everybody else's work. He says he's interested in having more time for himself and he's not going to spend all his life working anymore. He's got other things to do with his life. I'm not sure his behavior has much to do with his life. You know, he and I have moved up pretty fast in the last few years and I think it's making his head swim. He never thought he'd get this far. On the other hand, sometimes he acts like he's too good for us. I don't know. Maybe when he can't see the big picture - and what the purpose of all this is. Mostly when I see him, I just get angry and say, "Go to hell." It's interfering with my work though because I haven't anybody to talk things through with - and I'm sending my reports straight through the system instead of meeting with Dave. Something's really wrong with that guy."

After describing his conversation with Jim, Bob said that that was only part of the story. Bob thought maybe Jim was just having a bad day - but then maybe something **was** wrong with Dave. So Bob called Dave up and the two men had lunch. Dave looked fine, not tired or strung out, and seemed to be in good spirits. He was driving a new car and was glad to see Bob. They talked about football for a while. Then Bob asked him how he and Jim were getting along. Dave said calmly, "Jim? Oh, he's fine." When I encouraged him to talk a little more, he changed the subject. A few minutes later, however, Jim happened to walk past our table, nodded at me, scowled at Dave, and kept on going. Dave looked downcast. He started talking about Jim.

Dave's story: "That man's an idiot! We've worked together for years and look how he treats me. He walks right by without saying hello. You know, Jim has been different lately. A few months back he took credit for a report we both wrote. The VP called Jim up and said, "What a great report!" And Jim didn't say we'd worked on it together. He didn't admit I had anything to do with it. I guess I'm tired of being pushed around by him. Jim thinks he has such great ideas. He's aiming to be a star around here. You know, when the next promotion comes through at headquarters, there's only one place -- instead of the two we have now. I should have that promotion but Jim will get it instead. That's OK, you know. Let him devote his life to the company. Me, I want to enjoy life a little. And I'm not going to work with an SOB that takes credit for everything I do. You know, the other day, Jim drives all the way over to my office, comes inside, asks me a few questions, and then starts yelling at me. Hell, I've got too much living to do to spend my time being yelled at by guys who only think of getting ahead. I'm going to enjoy myself."

Bob said, "Now, Mark, you know both of them. What can we do. Work's *slowing down around here. Today, some of Jim's men refused to talk to Dave's crew. Just now I heard several of them say they were going to send all their work right on to headquarters instead of routing it through Dave's office like they usually do. When I talked to Jim last week, I wanted to make this system better. But it seems it's getting worse instead."*

Mark called Dave's manager and asked him to come to a meeting with both Jim and Dave. Mark was aware his options were limited. Due to economic retrenchment, all promotions and transfers were on hold for an unspecified period of time. Further, the procedure for actually terminating employment for individuals without a long record of incompetence was very lengthy and complicated. Unless the problem was of huge proportions, he knew both men should stay where they were now. As the meeting opens, Mark is aware of Jim's anger. Jim sits in his chair, banging his pen against the edge. Dave, on the other hand, appears slightly detached but calm. Dave is smiling slightly. What does Mark do now?

CIRCULAR AND CONICAL PHASES OF THE CHANGE PROCESS

The following sets of questions may be useful to you in checking out your own ideas and preparing to implement new ideas in order to better manage the change process. The questions are addressed to those in a work setting but can be used to think through problems in any area of your life.

I. Circular Phase: Clarifying Problems and Generating Alternatives
   -What is the surface nature of the problem?
   -What are the probable causes?
   -What would be the desired outcome?
   -What are alternative routes to achieving the desired outcome?
II. Conical Phase: Arriving at a Strategy for Success
   A. Significance of possible outcomes
      -Would the expected outcome have effects that will still make a difference in six months? 1 year? 2 years?
      -Would the expected outcome affect only your unit? or other units as well?
      -Would the expected outcome result in increased resources for the

unit in six months? 1 year? 2 years?

-Would the expected outcome result in increased productivity for the unit in six months? 1 year? 2 years?

-Would the expected outcome result in increased morale for the unit in six months? 1 year? 2 years?

-Could any increases in resources, productivity or morale be negated by other effects either inside our outside your own unit?   If   yes, detail what these other effects might be.

-Overall, summarize the benefits that would result for your unit if the plan were implemented.

B. Feasibility of implementation

-Are the resources necessary for implementation available within your unit? Outside your unit? Unavailable?

-Are the persons who control the resources identified? Are these individuals likely to give approval to your project?

-Have you identified other persons whose approval is necessary in order to implement your plan? Are these individuals likely to give their approval to your project?

-Have you identified all individuals who will be affected by implementation of this plan? Have you decided how and when they will be informed of this project? Have you decided to what degree their acceptance of the plan is necessary for successful implementation?

-What other possibilities might interfere with the implementation of your plan? Have you prepared contingencies for these possibilities?

-Overall, summarize the likelihood of implementing this particular plan.

Ten:
Playing the Game
with Changing Rules

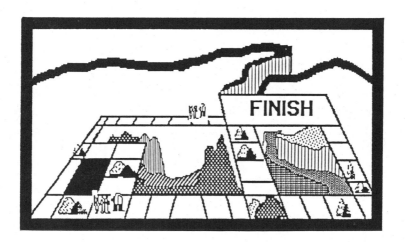

Encouraged by the idea of bringing together the players from the different parts of the gameboard, the travelers went first to the valleys to ask the players there to think about new ways to use the power of the wind. Imagining freely as was their habit, these players finally suggested that the winds, properly channeled, might be used to raise water from the streams, clean areas long clogged by debris, and eventually might provide the power to light up all gameboards! Amazed at the audacity of their own thoughts, these players drifted away to their usual pursuits, knowing that such an idea would never come about.

The travelers, however, drew up plans from these ideas and carried them to the hills where they asked those players if they would like help in bringing water to their shelters, in clearing away the underbrush, and in seeing in the dark. As the players of the hills looked dumbfounded, murmuring "It is not possible on our hill," the travelers unrolled the plans they had brought with them, declaring, "If you will do each of these steps, then you will have water, open ground, and possibly even light in the dark."

Reluctantly at first, the players of the hills began to argue about the plan: pointing out omissions, discussing unworkable steps, and substituting better ones. Working in a small group, hunched over the plans, they made a mark here and there, crossed out a section, and scratched in a new one. Finally, they thrust the plans at the travelers, grumbling, "Now it will work!" Surprised at their own words, unwilling to acknowledge that they had fleshed out a **new** *idea, they backed off slowly, turning to the* *task at hand. . .*

With the encouragement of the travelers, the players in the hills and valleys thought of more ideas and sketched out more plans. Gradually, as time wore on, players from the hills went to the valleys to check out details and players from the valleys went to the hills to propose a new idea. As the players went back and forth, the found that their differences were not as negative as they had feared . . . In fact, their differences were the basis of a profitable working relationship . . .

A department in the large division of a manufacturing concern began to change, and people started to work more enthusiastically and energetically than they had for years. They started to believe they were making the organization as a whole more effective. However as time went on they noticed that other departments were following the old *status quo* - relatively inefficient performance - and were suffering no negative consequences. The "energetic" department began to taper off its own efforts. Their attitude became one of "why bother?"

A manager in a different company worked out the way in which his parts were supplied so that he had an even workflow throughout the week. His people were pleased. Within two weeks, however, he was receiving angry memos from the managers of other departments. "Why are you messing up our schedules?" they wanted to know. The new and more efficient schedule initiated by the first manager had disrupted the familiar, if inefficient, schedules of other departments.

Each of the above examples shows that change occurring

in one part of a system does not occur in isolation, but affects the whole larger system. In this way an organizational structure is like a fishnet - whether large or small, an organization is composed of many interrelated focal points, just as a net is composed of interwoven knots. When any one focal point is changed - moved in one direction or another - it affects all the other focal points in the system, just as moving any knot changes the shape of the fishnet. Consequently, prospective changes must be examined in terms of their potential effects on the entire system.

Additionally, each part of a system has a specific history, and each has future possibilities that can only be guessed at in the present. Thus as the change process moves along its own time line, it affects aspects of the organization shaped by the past and, in turn, shapes the course of the future. Change, therefore, not only affects all of the system in the present, but redirects the course of that system as it moves from the past to the future (see Figure 10.1).

Difficulties in the Change Process

Many of the difficulties that emerge in the change process occur because all groups within a system are interrelated; while some may arise within the unit initiating change, some can result from issues external to the unit itself.

Problems which arise within the unit initiating change may be symbolized by the threads of a knot in the fishnet simply letting go - so that the knot is loosened and all connecting threads come apart. The project which might have been the focus of a unit's attention and activity for a time slowly moves into the background and the changes that might have occurred are no longer on the agenda. There are several reasons why this happens.

Most of these reasons stem from a *lack of belief* in the projected outcome and therefore a *lack of commitment* to the process. Individuals did not really believe that the change was possible: they say things such as "well, we never could have done it anyway," or "everybody knows that you can't change the system." As a consequence of the fragility of their belief, people did not really make a strong commitment to the process. A frequent occurrence is for people to be committed "as long as everything goes along as planned" but at the first sign of difficulty they bow out. When tentative beliefs and commitments are challenged by being put to work, people will often give up and give in.

Still other difficulties may kill a project along the way. A *lack of commitment* on the part of some individuals may lead to the dwindling away of the project in the planning phase, as they drift away from the focus of change. The perceived lack of energy is usually the result of energy being given to other things instead of the change process - and leads back to a lack of strong commitment in the initial phase and a lack of clearly established priorities in the planning phase.

Finally, a *lack of vigilance* in monitoring the process may allow many individuals to follow parallel paths and duplicate effort, so that the final result is of less significance to the system. Maintaining vigilance - a continuous focus on the process - requires persistence and perseverance, often in the face of difficulties, until the final goal is achieved. Such perseverance, built upon strong commitment in the first phase and clear priorities in the second, is essential for carrying through the third phase of implementation (see Figure 10.2).

Figure 10.1

THE EFFECTS OF ANY CHANGE

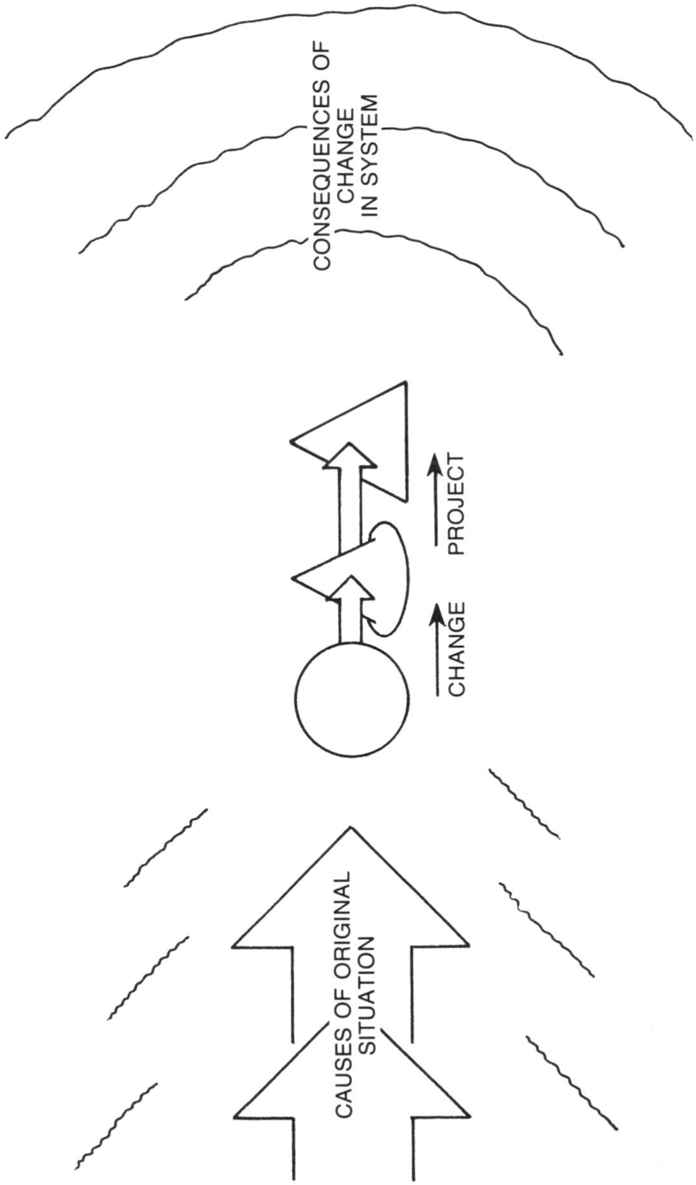

Figure 10.2

PROBLEMS ENCOUNTERED IN THE CHANGE PROCESS

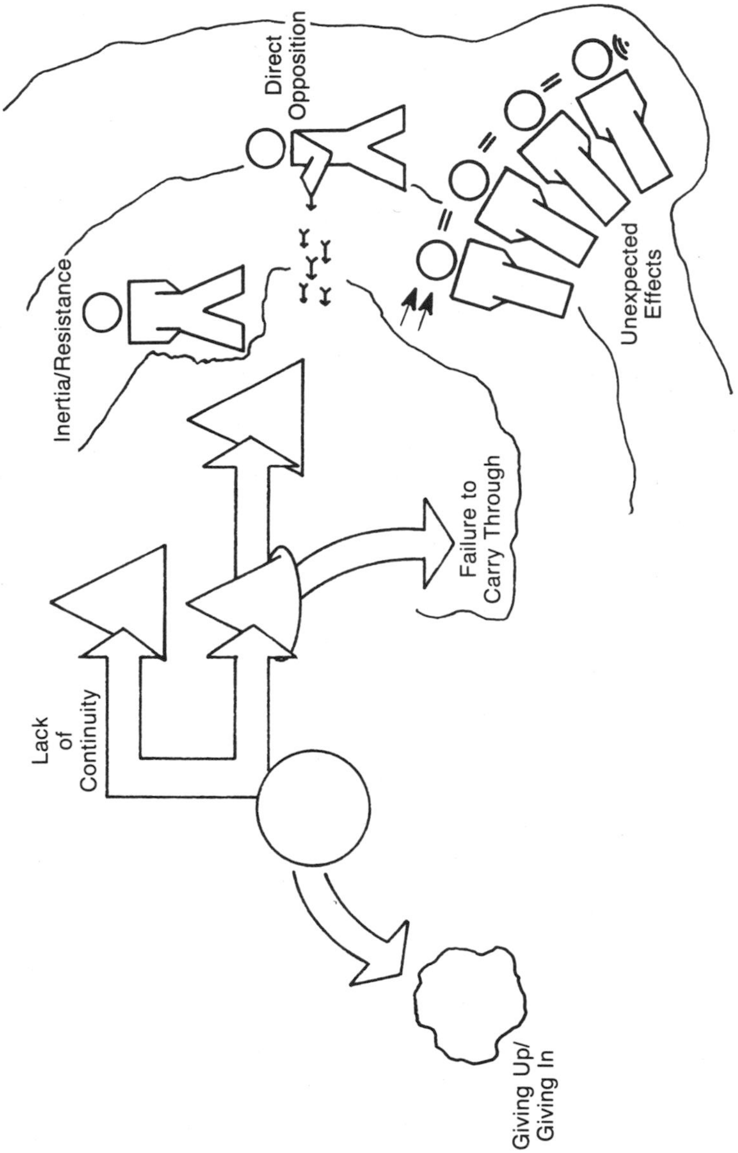

Other reasons for difficulty are *external* but can be overcome if sufficient belief, commitment, energy, and vigilance are present in the individuals initiating change. However if any of these characteristics are lacking, the change project may fade away in the face of external deterrents which can take any of several forms.

Almost all change efforts meet with inertia or *passive resistance* on the parts of at least some individuals. Most of us are not thrilled by the prospects of change, particularly when initiated by others, and at any given moment may sit rocklike in its path, causing its currents to move around us or to come to a halt altogether.

Some change efforts run into more *active resistance,* eliciting direct opposition from some individuals or units - and this resistance must be either diffused or combatted in order for change to proceed. Finally, some change efforts are forestalled by the *unexpected effects* of the actual change process on individuals who had seemed initially peripheral to the particular project. For example, the use of resources in one area may diminish the supply in another, arousing anger and resentment from another unit with the power to block change. Such unexpected effects sometimes can not be foreseen in advance but often are the result of inadequacies in the planning process in which certain results of change were not accounted for and *all* individuals to be effected were not consulted about the project (see Figure 10.2).

Thus change efforts may die from one or more difficulties which arise internally or externally to the unit initiating change. Internally, change efforts may fail because of a variety of deficiencies within those initiating change: a lack of belief and commitment; a failure to establish clear priorities that keep energy focused on the task; or a lack of persistence throughout the process which supports a vigilant monitoring of the change process itself.

Externally, a project may become vulnerable to external opposition to such an extent that the opposition overwhelms the degree of belief, commitment, energy, vigilance and persistence within the unit. The project may then be cancelled or allowed to drift off center stage. Outside resistance has overpowered internal determination to bring about change.

Such difficulties can be forestalled or overcome when individuals (1) believe in the possibilities inherent in change; (2) are willing to make a commitment to the process of change; (3) establish clear priorities so that energies are focused on the task; (4) are willing to monitor the change process with attentiveness; and (5) are willing to stand their ground and carry through despite difficulties that may surface throughout the process.

Guiding the Change Process

As players on our own organizational gameboards, all of us have been affected by the winds of change. In the work of each of us, the rules and the players have changed - more than we might have expected when we first entered the game. The choices that face us are only two: we can be buffeted by the winds of change, at the mercy of external forces and liable to be bounced from the game at any point; or we can guide the change process itself, initiating and carrying through changes that increase the survival probabilities of our own gameboard. The choice of staying as we are has been swept away by a turbulent environment. We may allow ourselves to be controlled by forces outside of ourselves or we may make that control our own - through belief, commitment, energy, vigilance and perseverance.

As masters of the change process we may build flexible organizations - the only ones able to survive in changing times - which have the following characteristics: (1) a balance between pyramidal and circular structures; (2) support for individuals working together in productive teams; (3) encouragement for new and emerging leadership among those who are willing to evaluate themselves and their organizations, to give up that which is no longer functional, and to create new systems that are responsive to current circumstances; and fourth, emerging leadership in the organization will call forth from others the best that they have to offer, so that ultimately leadership is found among individuals and groups throughout the organization.

Within such flexible organizations, all personality styles would have an appropriate place, pyramidal and circular structures would be matched to the demands of each task, changing as demanded by internal or external factors. Individual rewards in such an organization are drawn from the excitement of participating in the change process, in the satisfaction of overcoming difficulties, and in the knowledge that each one has a part to play in guiding the process of change. This, in fact, is essential for both individual satisfaction and organizational productivity - to grow comfortable with the process of change which, as far as anyone can see, will characterize the rest of our working lives and be most descriptive of the state of our organizations.

EXERCISE:
IMPLEMENTATION OF CHANGE PROJECTS

If you have arrived at some things you would like to change in your organization, you may want to draw up an action plan. Often, managing change requires that individuals persuade others to join with them in this effort. Consequently, they may often need to present their ideas to others in order to win their support. A model for such presentations follows, which you may choose to use in order to prepare a presentation or to clarify for yourself the goals and purposes, the significance and feasibility of your project. The last part presents a model for reviewing, after a period of time, any action you have undertaken. It also provides some useful reminders for areas to be particularly aware of as you manage the process of change.

Presentation Format

1. Identification of goal
    a. Nature of problem
    b. Specific plan of action
2. What steps will have been accomplished in the next five weeks? What are the short terms costs, if any? What are the short-term benefits?
3. What steps will have been accomplished in the next six months? What are the long-term costs, if any? What are the long-term benefits?
4. What do you see as the overall significance or importance of implementing this project? For your unit? For your division? For the corporation?

Project Action Plan Checklist

On completing your action plan, be sure your plan includes all the following checkpoints. If it does not, you may want to return to your plan and revise the steps to cover all possibilities.
1. Includes acquisition of all necessary resources
2. Includes securing approval from all individuals who have power to veto plan
3. Includes informing all individuals whose support will facilitate

implementation of plan

4. Breaks down steps into **measurable** components

5. Assigns **one** person responsibility for each step

6. Shares responsibility for all the steps among more than one or two individuals

7. Establishes realistic timetables for completion of each step

8. Includes method for assessing completion of each step

9. Provides contingency plans for lack of step completion (including alternative routes)

10. Provides recognition (and/or rewards) for step completion

11. Provides opportunities for monitoring progress and redefining steps as necessary

12. Provides opportunities for evaluation of project by all involved

Analysis of Completed Projects

When you have completed a change project, you may want to use the following outline as a guide to analyzing what you have accomplished - and planning your next project.

1. Original goal and brief statement of plan:

2. Steps accomplished and comparison with original goal:

3. Areas of greatest success (steps of action plan, particular project areas or specific individual efforts):

4. Areas of least success:

5. Most likely causes of lack of success (internal factors such as lack of time, energy, and commitment or external factors such as inertia, resistance, or opposition):

6. Benefits developing from involvement in project:

7. Liabilities incurred in development of project:

8. Modifications planned for future project involvement:

9. Most significant learnings from involvement in project:

Eleven:
Learning and Growing and Winning the Game[1]

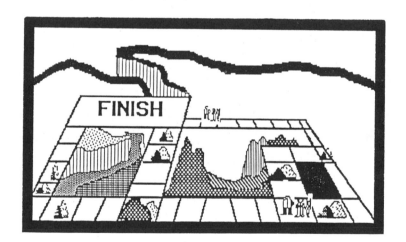

FINISH

This chapter was co-authored by Barbara Kovach, Glenn Morris and Randy Kovach.

All the players in the game are now travelers moving from start all the way to finish, comfortable in both the hills and valleys, with easy access to drinking water, paths clear of underbrush and light to see on gloomy days and dark nights. Yet this state of affairs was not reached quickly or easily . . . For after a spurt of initial enthusiasm those in the hills and valleys had fallen back to their old ways and there was a danger that the winds of change would once again be let loose on the gameboard, effectively stopping the game.

The change-oriented travelers met again to share their concerns and began a series of programs designed to minimize the stress that other players felt in adopting new ways and playing the game by new rules. In update sessions, the travelers reminded the others and themselves of the dangers attendant on not managing the change process. In training sessions, travelers and other players worked together to learn about themselves and each other and to recognize the opportunities inherent in each new problem on the gameboard.

Over time all the players came to accept that not only must they live with **these** *new rules but with changing rules for the rest of the game - and that security did not rest in a place or a task but in their own ability to play a game with changing rules and changing players in which the goal was for all players to win . .*

All of us are coping with change on a continuous basis. All organizations - and all managers - are responding to the forces of change occurring on cultural, economic and social levels. As this change occurs old boundaries shift and new ones form, and as organizations shift their boundaries, so must individuals change their own personal perspectives. Thus change has come to be viewed as a primary stressor, and it is how individuals respond to change, how they choose to play the game, that determines their potential for illness or for health for psychological retreat or personal growth. The tension an individual experiences between self and organization can create chronic conflict and distress, or can alternately motivate a person to change the organization or the self in a beneficial way. The tension resulting from the discrepancy between expectations and reality can prompt a person to assume a leadership role in guiding the process of change. In this chapter we shall review the forces that are creating change in organizations, the way that individuals may profitably respond to such change, and the new imperative for leadership that is emerging in these times of change.

Cultural Change

The world looks very different now than it did ten years ago - at least to most individuals in organizations. Countries have drawn closer together forming a global commercial network with an international marketplace that now supercedes national and regional territories. At the same time, growth in technology has transformed the internal workings of business operations in industrialized cultures. Thus managers must respond not only to a new big picture on the international scene, but to a new "little picture" on the technical scene - involving attention to the small details of new operations. In each picture organizational boundaries have shifted, requiring personal boundaries to shift as well. Such new demands produce a tension within individuals that can be used for either good or ill.

Managers today must know much more than managers some years ago. They must have knowledge about the markets and peoples of other nations, while acquiring an understanding of the new technological capabilities within their own companies. No one manager can master all the required knowledge, and consequently needs input from other people about about both the large world and the small one. Management is becoming even more of a team effort than it has been in the past in that what one person used to do now takes two or more. And for teams to be effectives, individuals must learn to communicate well with each other. Changes in the demand for knowledge in the last several years have led, therefore, to changes in the demand for interpersonal skills. Individual managers must adapt not only to new cultural and technological demands but also to new demands on their interpersonal abilities. These demands would certainly be expected to create tension between individuals and their organizations, and this tension is commonly referred to as stress.

Individual Response to Change

What many refer to as stress can really be viewed as

change, and since everything changes over time, just being alive can be said to create stress. Stress is a natural fact of life for all of us, and anything that happens in our lives can be potentially stressful. Things that cause stress are usually called stressors, but it is not really the event or the stressor itself which causes stress, but how we react to it. How we think and respond determines whether we experience stress or the excitement of facing new challenges. The strategies with which we choose to respond to change also have an effect on whether or not we experience stress. Stress is the response we make to events and is reflected in our physical, mental and emotional states.

Contrary to popular belief, stress can be regarded in two ways: in a negative sense as *distress*, or anxiety, wear and tear on the mind and body; or in a positive sense as *eustress*, excitement and exhilaration, growth and satisfaction. How one responds to change determines whether one will experience distress or eustress.

Consider the life events you may have experienced recently. Suppose a child left home, or you transferred to a new community, got a divorce, or had trouble with in-laws. How you might think about these events, how you might respond to them, would determine your level of stress. There is evidence suggesting that the more such events you experience, the more likely you are to experience some form of psychosomatic illness. Other evidence, however, suggests that frequency of significant life events may not, in and of itself, produce medical symptoms, and that for some people, a higher frequency of changeful events is significantly associated with *lower* frequency of psychosomatic or medical symptoms. For individuals committed to finding long-term solutions to their problems and willing to work at it, a higher number of changeful events may simply provide more challenges and could be said to result in eustress. Such individuals may have low levels of stress related medical symptoms, and also understand practices of good management, and interpersonal relationships. Chances are they also excel at planning, problem solving, and decision making.

When one is confronted with change and/or the necessity of making changes in life, the willingness to take action, and to commit oneself to something that is meaningful is an essential component in preventing illness and in promoting physical and emotional well-being. Yet we all have opportunities to take control of our lives by determining the ways in which we respond to change. Let us look now at some personality characteristics that facilitate turning distress into eustress.

1. Willingness to share life experience with others acts as a buffer to stress in a number of ways. Such sharing engenders acceptance and trust, and also allows one to acquire a greater understanding of personal issues; in other words one becomes more sophisticaled and able to see the world from more than one point of view. Trusting others also tends to create environments in which others grow more trusting. Consequently, sharing experiences with others has often been associated with emotional stability, positive assertion, and even creativity. The individual who is willing to share with others exhibits strength of character, warmth and sincerity.

2. Openness to new experiences increases the probability that change will be accepted without fear. The person open to new ideas is more likely both to recognize the need for change, and to instigate change.

3. Ability to solve problems also tends to lower stress. Good analytical skills are at the root of problem solving, and help prevent people from jumping to incorrect conclusions or selecting inappropriate solutions. People with an analytical bent are more likely to figure out what the real source of a problem is and to select an appropriate and effective solution.

4. Ability to think in terms of complete systems and complex interfaces relates to the ability to solve problems, and also helps innoculate one against disabling stress. Patterns of relationship are perceived and one becomes able to see the big picture. Knowledge can be integrated from a wide variety of sources. Skills in pattern recognition and integration allow a person both to interpret what is happening currently and to better predict what may happen in the future. This is a valuable asset when dealing with change.

5. Ability to make decisions and accept responsibility for those decisions is a buffer against anxiety. Harry Truman's famous motto - "The buck stops here" - exemplifies this attitude. A person high on decision-making skills will consider alternatives and evaluate their probable effects before choosing a plan of action. The decision maker who is willing to withold judgement, evaluate alternatives on their merits, and take responsibility without placing blame is likely to make final decisions on the best possible information. Such a person is less likely to leap into situations with unexpected and unhappy consequences and less likely to experience the negative effects of change.

6. Finally, individuals willing to act and to pursue their own objectives - despite obstacles - show markedly fewer signs of distress than do other people. Such individuals are often able to accomplish multiple tasks and to enjoy stretching themselves as they do it them. Often they reach out for

change if none is forthcoming, because to them change represents a challenge.

As we all live in this time of tremendous social and economic change, we are all responsible for the perspective we bring to this age of transition. All of us have a responsibility to use the tensions resulting from change to enlarge our own worlds and those of others. Specifically in relationship to organizations, when individuals recognize and accept the tensions existing between their own expectations and those of the organization, they can use this discrepancy as motivation for both personal growth and organizational change. They can assume responsibility for creating new rules and continuing to play the game effectively.

Individuals and Organizations

In changing times, individuals experience different kinds of tension within their organizations. Some individuals who adapt relatively well to change are right in sync with their organizations and experience relatively little tension or distress. The pace of organizational change is right in step with their own personal rhythm. Other individuals, who are moderately or extremely out of sync with their organizations, tend to fall into two categories. Some of these individuals are *ahead* of their organizations in terms of desire for and adaptability to change; they tend to experience loss of this in their personal lives and to thrive on challenges. Thus, they may feel restricted by their organizations and impatient with their colleagues, often urging them to learn better communication skills and open up more with each other.

In the second category of out-of-sync individuals are those who are *behind* their organizations in terms of desire for and adaptability to change. These individuals feel as if changes are moving too quickly for them, leaving them in limbo and without guidelines. They lag behind demanding of their organizations that they establish rules, procedures, and guidelines for times of transition, and that caution be exercised in attempting the new or sidelining the old.

Surprisingly, all three groups of individuals - the one in sync *and* the two out of sync with their organizations - are essential to the organizational change process. Those who experience only moderate tension around the change process usually emerge as central leaders, shaping and monitoring the integration of new programs with old ones. Those experiencing tension when the organization does not move quickly enough champion new programs, create new procedures, and insist on training and development to help promote organizational change. Those experiencing tension when the organization moves too quickly for them argue for caution, scrutinize new programs, and insist that rules and procedures be developed to channel the course of change. Each group provides a balance for the others as organizations come to terms with the new realities of a changing world.

That is, each provides a balance for others *when they choose to do so*. Often individuals sit back when faced with disparity between personal and organizational expectations, hoping that the organization will do something for them - only to experience the negative effects of tension, stress as distress. Individuals who act to decrease tension through both personal and organizational change, while doing something for the organization, often experience eustress, the positive side of tension, as challenge and excitement. Because their response to change is positive and constructive, they place themselves in control of the process of change.

In the following examples, individuals demonstrate decidedly different responses to the changes occurring in their organizations. From in sync and out of sync positions, each of these three men contributed to the welfare of the same organization.

John Paulson is in sync with his organization. He works for a large company moving toward participative management, which he perceives to reflect a balance of pyramids and circles; an Integrator himself, he is comfortable with this. As the organization has moved to create change within itself, Mr. Paulson has found himself assuming a formal leadership role in guiding the process. He is pleased with the pace of change for it suits his own.

Tom Hanover is out of sync with this same organization and experiences tension between his own expectations and those of his company. He perceives his organization as becoming more circular with communication and teamwork receiving new emphasis, while he continues to prefer focusing on getting the work done. As far as he is concerned, must of this new emphasis is "crap." At first bitter about the direction of the organization, he retreated into his own work area and focused solely on his job; eventually, however, he was drawn into a number of planning meetings and became an important influence in making sure that new procedures and systems are carefully thought through and understood before implementation. Mr. Hanover is a Producer in a conical environment.

Arnie Matthews is also out of sync with this organization, finding himself frustrated by what he perceives as a lack of change. Obviously, his perception is not shared by either John Paulson or Tom Hanover, and they all work for the same company. Mr. Matthews, always on the go, wanders around talking to people and creating new ideas for product lines. He actively pursues change and is impatient for his organization to catch up. Recently, he has become influential in getting new training programs begun and in opening up channels of communication between subordinates and their bosses. Rather like a gadfly, he continually reminds others that they cannot be complacent with the changes that have occurred already, for there are more to come. Mr. Matthews is a Processor in the midst of organizational change.

Individuals experiencing tension and acting to create change are informal change agents within organizations. Such individuals distinguish themselves by communication skills and by their ability to work with groups of people. Because they listen well, they understand other peoples' point of view; because they know themselves, they are also able to communicate clearly their own. Such individuals become centers of influence within organizations; they are the players who survive on a constantly changing gameboard. Depending on their own degree of fit, they may urge organizations to open up communication channels, to develop clear guidelines for transition, or may become spokespersons for the organization's central direction. In any case, their influence and ability to guide change rests on their ability to communicate and to work with others. Out of these characteristics comes their leadership potential.

The Leadership Imperative

If we are to survive through the next tumultuous decades, it is incumbent upon all of us to develop our leadership potential and to take control of the process of change. Each of us must throw ourselves, without reserve, into the game and not out of it. Organizations that survive and prosper will have within them many individuals who are centers of influence, and who focus attention on the need for continuity as well as the need for change. Organizations that fail to survive and/or prosper will have within them many individuals who continually give up their own influence to others, and who wait for someone else to do something for them.

In order for each of us to increase our own leadership potential, we need to strengthen our abilities to work well with others. We need to know our own minds and how to speak them, and also know when to be silent and listen to others. When we do both of these things, we have the information on ourselves and our environment that will help us to make the best decisions in any given situation. We will have amassed the fullest array of facts and opinions from our associates, while understanding more fully our own point of view, and on that basis will be able to make decisions responsibly and to accept the consequences. We will have become leaders within our own particular groups, large or small, the players who survive in any game, no matter what the rules turn out to be.

Tension *can be* beneficial. Many of us would sit in the sun all day doing little else if our environments suited us in all ways; we tend to get up and do something because this is often not the case. *Because* our organizational environment differs from what we think it could be, many of us are actively involved in the change process - for us it is difficult to simply sit in the sun expecting others to make things better. We utilize the tension productively to improve our communication, better our teamwork, and act so as to bring our environments more in line with our expectations. To the extent that all of us develop our own potentials, we use the changes in our lives to create eustress (not distress) and move toward leadership positions in this time of change.

What this means in terms of the theme of this book is that as organizations move toward an integration of pyramids and circles, individuals themselves have to grow in order to profit from this integration. As the game evolves, so must the players. Producers must reach a level where they are comfortable in team settings, making the most of their potential for positive team contributions. Integrators must use their talents to help others achieve rather than focusing exclusively on themselves, and must create the systems and the procedures that provide some stability in times of change. Processors must stop talking and start doing something, often charting the direction in which change will move. All Producers, Integrators and Processors, in fact, can choose a path of personal growth rather than one of retreat. They can use their own tensions in the face of change to create better organizations that balance caution and innovation, consistency and flexibility, continuity and change. By choosing to become part of the change process rather than retreating from it, they can weave into the organizational fabric a new balance between pyramids and circles. They will then create the organizations that will insure America's rightful place as a player to be reckoned with on the international gameboard.

EXERCISE:
YOU, BELIEF SYSTEMS, AND CHANGE CAPABILITY

Follow the directions below in order to estimate your degree of tension with your organization, the direction of that tension, and your capacity to enact change in your environment.

Belief Systems
Organizational

To find the **degree of tension** that you experience around the issues of organiztional change, subtract your score on the **Mini-Personality Expecta-tions Inventory** (pp. 49-51) from your first score on the **Mini-Organization-al Expectations Inventory** (pp. 34-35). If the resulting number falls between +2 and -2, you experience only a moderate degree of tension about change. If the number is greater than +2 or less than -2, you experience a cor-respondingly greater degree of tension around the issues of organizational change.

To find the **direction** in which you think the organization should move in order to minimize your tension, notice the + or - sign preceding the number indicating degree of tension. Interpret this in the following manner:

A + sign indicates that you believe the organization would become more effective if everyone knew what the expectations of the organization were at this time and if the rules and procedures of the organization were applied consistently across the board. Individuals who have a high degree of tension preceded by a + may either (1) believe that their organization is moving too quickly in a participative direction and that more caution and some return to "the old ways" of management is necessary; or (2) agree with new participative trends in their organization but believe that more rules and regulations, consistently applied, should accompany the transition to prevent individuals from feeling as if they are operating in limbo; or (3) believe that their organization is basically spineless and unable to develop coherent policies with which to transact business.

A - sign indicates that you believe the organization would become more effective if individuals learned to communicate better, develop more effective teams, and in general pay more attention to indivuals within the organization. Some individuals with a high degree of tension around change and a - preceding the tension number may be impatient for new worlds that they can envision but are far from being enacted in most organizational settings.

Group

To find the **degree of tension** that you experience in interaction with your immediate work group subtract your score on the **Mini-Personal Expectations Inventory** (pp. 49-51) from your score on the **Mini-Group Expectations Inventory** (pp. 84-86). If the resulting number falls between +2 and -2, you experience only a moderate degree of tension in interaction with your work group. If the number is greater than +2 or less than -2, your experience a correspondingly greater degree of interaction with your work group.

To find the **direction** in which you believe you or your work group should move in order to minimize this tension, notice the + or - sign preceding the number indicating degree of tension. Interpret this in the following manner:

A + sign indicates that you believe your group is more open to change than you yourself are. It may mean that you are hurrying to catch up with your group and that they, in fact, are leading the way into a more open style of management. On the other hand, you may believe that your group is wild and unruly and that they would be better served by a more conscientious attention to organizational rules, procedures and expectations.

A - sign indicates that you believe your group would profit from improving their communication and teamwork skills. You, yourself, are probably more open to change than they and are impatient for them to catch up. Sometimes these scores indicate that you would like your group to be more open **with you** and may wonder, in fact, why they do not share as much of their experience with you as you would like.

Change Capability

Use your change capability score from the **Mini-Personal Presentation Inventory** (pp. 103-104) to determine how you respond to the degree of tension which you experience in your organization or with your work group. Use the chart below to determine your probable response to varying degrees of tension according to the degree of change capability.

Change Capability	Degree of Tension	
	Moderate	**High**
Low	You are probably relatively content with the current state of affairs in your organization or your group. In general, expectations of your behavior are set by others, but they accord with what you would like for yourself and you experience little need to change things.	You are probably experiencing considerable stress with your organization and/or work group and feel powerless to change things. You may feel somewhat like a victim in your current organizational setting.
Moderate	You are probably relatively content with the current state of affairs in your organization or your group. In some areas, you have assisted in establishing expectations for your behavior and that of others and believe that your efforts make some difference, but in other areas you accept things the way they are whether you like them or not.	You are probably experiencing considerable tension between your organization and/or group and yourself and, in some areas, are actively trying to change things to fit your own belief system. In some areas, however, you feel you can do little to affect change and are sometimes resentful and/or bewildered by the way these areas operate.
High	You are probably relatively content with the current state of affairs in your organization or your	You are probably experiencing considerable tension between your organization, your work

group. The reason you are pleased is that you have had a large hand in shaping the expectations that govern your environment. If you believe something is not operating in the best way possible, you act so as to improve the situation. In most situations, you find yourself feeling "at home," since you are a strong influence on designing these situations and they are often created to fit your own beliefs and expectations.

group, and/or yourself, but you are enjoying the challenges that this tension provides and enthusiastic about the opportunities for changing things in ways you believe will be more effective. It is not likely that you will remain in this environment for long without diminishing the tension between you and the organization, for you will bring others along your own path.

Direction of Change

Combine your interpretative summaries for the **direction** of change with those given under change **capability** to have an estimate of the areas in which you experience the most stress or are making the greatest change efforts. It is clear to us that stress and change efforts are usually mutually exclusive. If we experience stress because of disparities between ourselves and our environment, we are often brooding about the differences rather than acting to make them less. If we are working for change, on the other hand, we are often motivated and exhilarated by the discrepancies between our expectations and those of others and are, by our own efforts, likely to diminish these discrepancies.

Appendix

Case Histories and Exercises

The following case histories and exercises have been used extensively by our consulting company, Human Systems Analysis, Inc., in our work with Rochester Products Division of General Motors from 1982 to 1987. All of the case histories were written to describe incidents described to us in our initial work with this General Motors division or our work at Ford Motor Company from 1981 to 1982.

Although the case histories reflect a manufacturing and/or technical setting, each one was used to elaborate on the general principles described throughout this book. The stories and exercises are, thus, grouped and identified according to related chapters. Readers may find them useful in gaining a greater understanding of their own work experience. Those wishing to use these materials in group settings may contact Human Systems Analysis, Inc., for the materials specifically designed for management and supervision training sessions.

The case histories and exercises, as presented here, are designed to assist individual readers in understanding themselves, others and their own organization. Answers and commentaries for each exercise follow at the end of this section.

Section One:
Identifying the Players

Exercises and Case Histories
Related to
Chapter 4
Players as Producers, Integrators and Processors

IDENTIFYING PERSONALITY PATTERNS

Under each of the descriptions below, identify the most likely personality style of each person described.

John P. is a 58-year old first-line supervisor who has been with the company over 30 years. He is known for meeting his quotas and getting the job done. He can be seen any day walking around on the plant floor checking production and commenting on efficiency. When a machine breaks down, he yells at the men until it is fixed. He tells them each day that the work must get done, no matter what. He is careful about getting his schedule out and posts them prominently. "As long as we stay on schedule," he says, "we will be the best unit in the plant."

John is most likely a Producer   _____
                    Integrator   _____
                    Processor   _____

Allen O. is a 54-year-old manager of an engineering unit. He has been with the company over 20 years. He acquired his present position 10 years ago and will hold it until retirement. Allen is warm and friendly to everyone entering his office. He talks openly about his problems with anybody who come in. Frequently he can be seen in the offices of his subordinates, chair tipped back, feet on their desk, discussing work - and fishing and other common interests. His subordinates report that they always feel better after talking with Allen. But, they also say, his meeting are too long and rambly because he never follows an agenda and he talks a long time about every topic that comes up. Many people say they really admire Allen O. but some others say they can't get along with him because he never follows a schedule and is always cahanging his mind.

Allen is most likely a Producer   _____
                    Integrator   _____
                    Processor   _____

Arthur P. is a 32-year-old engineer who is reputed to be the best engineer in the entire unit. When something doesn't work, everybody always asks Arthur what to do. He comes up with quick, simple and workable solutions. Arthur likes his work and often retires to his own engineering room where he can organize his equipment and work on his favorite projects. He resists going to meetings and feels they are a waste of time. He was passed over for a promotion four years ago because he "didn't want to play politics" and refused to go along with his boss on several projects. He believes that he has been unjustly treated because his work is superior and yet others have passed him by. All that counts, he says, is doing your job right. The rest is b___ s___ .

Arthur is most likely a Producer   _____
                    Integrator   _____
                    Processor   _____

Tom H. is a 35-year-old General Supervisor who has been promoted quickly. Others are sometimes resentful of his position - and complain about his loud voice and his insistence on getting the job done. Tom does talk loudly and is inclined to bark out orders when a crisis occurs. Other times, however, he can be seen talking with his subordinates and giving them lots of encouragement in their work. In talking with Tom, it is clear that he is focused on "making the unit productive," and that he is willing to change schedules and sometimes make exceptions in procedures in order to get the work done. He is strongly concerned that "his people feel like a team" and is spending time with some of the people who feel left out and encouraging them to participate more fully in the unit. His subordinates appreciate him for his interest - and yet are still aware that he is a hard-taskmaster. They sometimes talk among themselves about how Tom is overly ambitious and could easily kill them all with overwork if they let him get away with it.

Tom is most likely a Producer   _____
               Integrator   _____
               Processor   _____

Alice S. is a first-line supervisor in a manufacturing plant. Prior
to coming to the plant, she had been a supervisor in an office and
in a retail establishment. She is 39 years old and plans to make her
career at the plant, hoping to move up to General Supervisor at
some time. Alice is dependable, responsible and gets the work
done. She spends less time talking with her people than some other
supervisors but more time in actually monitoring their work. She
prepares schedules for the week. She takes time to check the work
at the end of the day and carefully records production totals. She
notices when work is incorrectly performed and speaks immediately to the person involved. Sometimes, she takes over a machine and
shows the other person how to do the work. It sometimes seems
as if she likes doing the work herself almost better than directing
others. Her people think highly of her, however, even though they
sometimes wish she would take more personal time with them. Yet
they are aware that they can count on fair treatment from Alice.

Alice is most likely a Producer	_____
Integrator	_____
Processor	_____

PERSONALITY PATTERNS IN INTERACTION

Tom H. is an Integrator and, as General Supervisor, has two first-line
supervisors working for him who are both Producers, John P. and Alice S.
Tom has very high expectations for his supervisors and is sometimes
frustrated when they do not work as hard as he would like them to. John
and Alice, however, are very effective in getting the job done on a day to
day basis. What do you think would be some areas in which Tom would be
disappointed in their performance? Why?

Place a check next to as many of the areas listed below as you believe
would be likely areas of disappointment for Tom in his supervision of John
and Alice:
    a. ___ Hands-on knowledge of their operations
    b. ___ Being able to step in and help out when something goes wrong

   c. ___ Setting clear expectations about production schedules
   d. ___ Delegating authority for routine decisions to employees
   e. ___ Getting involved in longer-term planning and letting employees handle problems themselves
   f. ___ Taking an advisory capacity in relation to employees rather than simply directing them in their work

Allen O. is a Processor and manager of an Engineering Unit. One of his Engineers is Arthur P., a Producer. Allen and Arthur have worked together for over eight years. They are frequently angry with each other. Arthur says Allen is a dictator, steals ideas and doesn't recognize good work. Allen says Arthur has too small a picture of what is required of him and doesn't understand the total operation. In a discussion in which they tried to define "technical competence" they came to understand each other better - because they both viewed competence in very different ways. Which statements do you think Allen would have made and which would have been Arthur's?

Identify each statement by writing the name of one of the men in the space provided. Technical competence means:
   a. ___ the ability to understand different aspects of scientific theory
   b. ___ the ability to find the simplest and least costly solution to an immediate problem
   c. ___ the operational knowledge to step in and fix any machine which breaks down
   d. ___ knowing how to look answers up in engineering books when you don't have the answer
   e. ___ being able to give specific instructions to the technicians on how to set up a test session
   f. ___ recognizing and using technical and scientific abilities in others

---

RESOLVING PERSONALITY CONFLICTS

The setting: A small high tech assembly line which is part of a larger manufacturing operation

Cast of Characters: Jack, Plant Manager
                   Harry, General supervisor

Susan, Supervisor
Bobby, Technician
Descriptions of Characters:

Jack has been successful in keeping a profit margin in the plant in uncertain economic times. He believes this is so because the plant delivers products of good quality and delivers them on time. He is willing to listen to new ideas and has rewarded his employees for coming up with new ways of doing things. He also believes in efficiency and has built good relationships with both the maintenance and quality assurance people so that his plant is run smoothly with a minimum of down time and scrap.

You will be Harry

Susan is highly regarded because she is good at organization and keeps the lines running smoothly. She plans her schedules carefully and is constantly checking on her employees to keep everybody on schedule. Three years ago she reorganized the line and gained a consistent 35% improvement in quality and production. She is considered a very good supervisor by her boss.

Bobby is a bright young technician working on an engineering degree. He often doesn't follow dress norms for the shop and usually has a transister radio plugged into his ear. He invented a new assembly technique last year which increased the product's capability and marketability without increasing the cost. His inventiveness is regarded as a company asset.

The Problem:

Susan has just discovered that there is a slowdown on the line and that the source of the slowdown seems to be Bobby. At 8:05 in the morning she bursts into your office. She is very angry and wants you to fire Bobby. She claims that he has been insubordinate, is blocking the line, and is undermining her authority. She waves some papers at you, saying that she has documented what she's saying. She shows you her notes from the last three days that tell when she discovered the problem on the line, how she found out that the source of the trouble was Bobby, and how he defied her and refused to change his behavior at her request.

At 8:30 Bobby drops by and sits comfortably in the chair across from your desk. He says offhandedly that Susan is harrassing him unfairly. He's been working on a new idea, is just about to get it right, but has met a stumbling block. When he discovered that his project was in trouble, he slowed down at his other work in order to think about it. He went on to say that Susan has let her title go to her head and is out to get him since he won't put up with her guff. He is working harder than anybody else, after all.

At 9:00 Jack calls and asks why the week's production totals are down. He stresses again the importance of maintaining the quality and efficiency of their production.

Working Toward a Solution:

I. Identify the probable personality styles of the main characters:

Bobby is probably a(n) _____

Susan is most likely a(n) _____ or maybe a _____

Jack is probably a(n) _____

II. Bobby's main strength lies in his _____

_____

Susan's main strength lies in her _____

_____

III. At 9:30 Harry calls both Susan and Bobby into his office. This is what he says to them:

_____

_____

_____

_____

_____

_____

IV. At 10:00 Jack calls back and asks Harry what he is going to do to get production back up. Harry tells him:

_____

_____

_____

_____

_____

_____

Will your solution solve the problem? Why or why not? If not, do you have an alternative solution? If so, what would it be?

WORKING FROM STRENGTH

Referring to the strengths identified by your **Personal Expectations Inventory** profile, list those strengths which you believe are are characteristic of you. Do not write in any characteristics with which you do not identify but only those which you recognize as characteristic of your own personality.

_____

_____

_____

_____

_____
_____
_____
_____
_____
_____

Now list below any additional characteristics which you perceive as your strengths:

_____
_____
_____
_____
_____

Desribe your current job:

_____
_____
_____
_____
_____

Describe the characteristics of your *desired* job either now or within the next two to five years:

_____
_____
_____
_____

What characteristics in addition to those you have are necessary for optimal performance in your current job?

_____
_____
_____
_____
_____

What characteristics in addition to those you have would be useful in order for optimal performance in your desired job? Are these different from those you just listed above?

_____
_____
_____
_____
_____

What people do you know who would "supply" these useful characteristics by joining your team and working with you? With which individuals might you share responsibility? To which individuals would you delegate specific functions?

_____
_____
_____

What else might you do to develop some of these characteristics in yourself or to acquire the materials/tools which would help you do this?

Section Two
Difficulties of Personal Change

Exercises and Case Histories
Related to
Chapter 2
The Process of Organizational Change

I GOTTA BE TOUGH

Bob J. was General Supervisor in the testing division of a major manufacturing company. Three first-line supervisors, one for each of three shifts, reported to him. In turn, these men supervised about 30 technicians. Bob J. was regarded as a hard-nosed, somewhat unfriendly supervisor. His men learned to avoid him if they had a problem or an idea about how to improve things. They felt it was quicker to fix the problem themselves than to have to answer Bob's questions and fill out his forms. They also believed that if they had an idea about how to do something better, Bob would turn it down - so there was little point in asking. They learned to run their own show and keep Bob out of it as much as possible.

Bob wondered why his men did not come to him with problems - but assumed that everything was going OK. He knew that, in the past, they used to come to him with ideas. He always listened to the ideas and thought them over. But generally, he was fond of saying, if somebody had one idea, another person had a contradictory one, so it was just better to do nothing. For Bob, new ideas seemed to cancel each other out. Also, if he accepted somebody else's idea, and didn't have a better one himself, they might think he was *dumb* and he wanted to avoid that at all costs. Bob consequently appeared to be *tough* in supervisory style, and, in this unit all the people problems were handled elsewhere. Bob busied himself with forms and instructions and assumed that the unit ran just fine.

Over a period of a few years, Bob went through several changes in his personal life. His sons left home, either to work or go to school, and his wife went back to work. He had less pressure on him at home and more time to think about his work. He began to wonder why people at work talked to him so little. He talked to some people, read some articles, and decided to make some changes in his style. Cautiously, he began to spend a little more time on the floor and occasionally traded jokes with his technicians. Occasionally, he commented on somebody's good work. Finally, he began asking people if they had any ideas about how to improve the operation. His first-line supervisors and technicians responded to these overtures with skepticism. Was he setting them up? What was going on? They continued with their old ways and wondered why Bob was around so much.

After a month or two of this behavior, the technicians, with the tacit approval of the supervisors, decided to test this new behavior on Bob's part and see what he would do. They began coming in later for work, they took longer lunches, and they spent less time in housekeeping chores. They did not come to attention when Bob made his rounds but rather waved at him casually and went back either to their conversations or their work. The testing rooms took a completely different atmosphere.

Bob was upset about what was happening. A few months earlier he would have called them in and they would have shaped up. But they wouldn't talk to him like they did now. Now, they no longer seemed to respond to his authority. He thought for several days about what to do.

If you were Bob which of the alternatives below would you prefer? Rank the alternatives from 1 to 6 with 1 being most preferred and 6 being least preferred.

a.___ Call the supervisors in and tell them to tighten the screws and get this place shipshape again.

b.___ Keep on with the new behavior but spend more time letting the technicians and first-line supervisors know that you keep proper hours, do your work, and clean up before leaving and expect them to do the same.

c.___ Call in the supervisors one by one and find out what is bothering them and why they are letting the place get sloppy about procedures.

d.___ Call a group meeting of supervisors and technicians and emphasize their responsibility to you - and the company - and lay out what will be the consequences of not complying with procedures.

e.___ Visit the work groups (which are already in progress) and help them set agendas for dealing with these problems and improving communication between them and the supervisors.

f.___ Form teams of both supervisors and technicians to establish clear quidelines for procedures and to develop ways to gain everybody's commitment on following the procedures.

Other alternatives:

_____

_____

_____

_____

Section Three
Acting as Managers and Supervisors

Exercises and Case Histories
Related to
Chapter 5
Players as Managers and Leaders

WHO'S TO BLAME?

In an assembly plant of an automobile factory, the employees worked under constant pressure to meet their quotas. Many times outdated machinery broke down and was repaired slowly so that an entire line was down for several hours. In addition, employees reacted to the stress by arguing with each other every time something went wrong. In one instance, two men argued with each other for a half-hour about whose fault it was that the machine broke, before they even called maintenance. In another instance, three employees refused to work for an hour because they said they were doing all the work and groups of other employees always got off easy and nobody ever made them do anything. Finally, one afternoon, eight men got into a loud argument around one machine, each of them yelling at the others that the reason things weren't working right was somebody else's fault.

Joe was the supervisor of this section. He had been on the job over fifteen years and had a reputation for getting things done. In September of 1979, the plant had a big order to complete that required the delivery of a large number of high quality parts in a short period of time. Many of the difficulties which occurred that month - problems with the machinery and the employees - slowed down production and the deadline was not met. On that occasion, Joe had called several members of the day shift into his office. Pounding on the desk, red in the face, he demanded to know "Who's to blame?" The workers said, "It's the machines, we can't get them repaired in time to meet our schedules." Joe shouted, "The **machines**! You're always looking for an excuse! If the work doesn't get done, it's your fault." His workers looked sullen and resentful as they left the office and went back to work.

The next month, in October, the plant had another tight deadline. The same section was having trouble meeting their schedules. Joe called the men into his office again and was prepared to chew them out. This time, however, he sat down first and thought about it. Were there other alternatives? he considered a number of different things he might do and say......

Rank the following alternatives in the order in which you think Joe should try them. Write a 1 to a 6 in front of each statement, with 1 indicating your first choice and a 6 indicating your last choice.

Joe might:

a.___ Continue to put the responsibility for lack of productivity on the men and give them the same talk as before so that they will understand the importance of meeting schedules under any conditions.

b.___ Show them that you have met your deadlines under any conditions (which is in fact true) by working at top speed when necessary and encourage them to do the same.

c.___ Talk to them individually and find out if they have personal or work problems which are keeping them from putting out their top effort.

d.___ Tell them as a group that they're trying their best - but they've got to do better - and that you'll help them out individually if together they will help you out.

e.___ Set aside some time for the men to talk to each other to sort out their differences and to decide how to solve their problems ahead of time instead of after the fact.

f.___ Set aside time for weekly meetings in which groups of workers can operate as a team to improve relationships among themselves and to consider ways to forestall further problems in the area.

After ranking the above alternatives, list any alternatives you think might better serve Joe's purposes than those listed.

_____

_____

_____

Identify which alternative above (a through f) is compatible with the managerial style listed below:

Chief_____

Patriarch_____

Counselor_____

Facilitator_____

Role Model_____

Team Leader_____

WHATEVER IT TAKES

In an assembly plant of an automobile factory, workers and supervisors worked overtime to meet their schedules. Tom was a first-line supervisor of one department. Bryan was his General Supervisor. Bryan had a reputation for being standoffish toward his Supervisors since he was not often available for suggestions, help or advice. Tom and others said that Bryan "kicked them when they were wrong" but never noticed when they were right.

In September of one year, business was especially heavy and Tom failed to meet his schedules. Bryan called him on the carpet and told him his job was defined as doing "whatever it takes" and he was clearly not handling the problems and getting the work out.

Tom stomped back to his department after this showdown. He was angry and resentful. He believed that it was not possible to work any faster. His workers didn't want to work: half of them just put in the required time with minimum effort and the other half grumbled because they had to do it all. Tom knew too that his machines were too old to produce the desired quality without hours and hours of sorting. He felt that he had few choices.

Nonetheless, the next day, Tom called his workers together and gave them a pep talk. He told them they had to work together to make their schedules or things would be pretty bad. He saw some of the workers snickering in the back of the meeting. He said nothing to them and left the meeting feeling that the situation would not get any better. In fact it did not. The next month, Tom's department again fell behind. Tom knew what was coming when Bryan called him into his office.

Tom's meeting with Bryan, however, was suddenly postponed when Bryan was called out of the plant on family business. Tom had a week to consider what he was going to say in his meeting with Bryan. He spent some time talking with other supervisors, with his better workers, and planning a new approach. He came up with six different ideas to present to Bryan.

Rank the six ideas below in the order in which you think Tom might present them to Bryan. Write a 1 to a 6 in front of each statement, with 1 indicating your first choice and a 6 indicating your last choice.

Tom might:

a.___ Supervise his workers continually, and discipline those workers who are slacking off.

b.___ Work side by side with his workers when he could, showing them that putting out more effort paid off in productivity.

c.___ Talk with the workers individually and ask them what he could do to improve their working situation so that more work might get done each day.

d.___ Hold a group meeting and tell the workers that they are doing OK but they must do better and that you'll help them out if together they will help you out.

e.___ Set aside some time for the workers to meet to draw up lists of suggestions for improving the productivity of the work force.

f.___ Establish weekly meetings with several groups of workers in which Tom and his people would analyze the situation and establish incentives and rewards for good work.

Write down any other alternatives below:

_____

_____

_____

_____

NOBODY TELLS US ANYTHING

Mark was a first-line supervisor in an automobile plant. He worked hard at his job which he felt was an almost impossible one. First line supervisors, he said, received the blame for anything that went wrong. Nonetheless, Mark - like many others - managed to get the work out and his department had a good reputation in the plant.

Lately, though, Mark was even less happy with his job. The supervisor who worked most closely with him was suddenly moved to another job. Mark heard about this in the lunchroom - he was not notified ahead. Then the new supervisor who was brought in was fresh out of college and Mark was responsible for his training. Again he was not warned ahead of time but rather learned from the new supervisor himself when he arrived. Then,

Mark heard that he was to be moved into Material Handling. The move did not entail a promotion but was a lateral move. Mark did not know if this were a "punishment" or a "reward." He was puzzled by all this and when his workers started giving him a hard time about some small issue, he simply turned his heel and walked away. Did anybody know what was going on here?

Mark's supervisor was away on business connected with the plant. When he was in town he was continually tied up in meetings. Mark's connections with the other supervisors were good but they didn't know any more than he did. His workers knew less than he did. What was he going to do next?

Rank the six alternatives below in the order in which you think Mark might try them. Write a 1 to a 6 in front of each statement, with 1 indicating your first choice and 6 indicating your last choice.

a.___ Resign himself to a bad situation, give up putting out extra effort to get the work done, and do just enough to draw down his salary.

b.___ Ask questions of people up the line until he got an answer and continue to get the work done, setting an example for his men.

c.___ Take his boss out for a drink at the first possible opportunity and ask if there is anything he can do to help <u>him</u> (the boss).

d.___ Call a meeting of his work force and tell them about the upcoming move and that they must continue to do a good job for the next guy that is coming in here and that he, Mark, would continue to be available for advice on various issues.

e.___ Call a meeting of all other supervisors in the plant so that the supervisors can work together to get more information, help each other in difficult situations, and suggest solutions for problems in the plant.

f.___ Work with other supervisors to sponsor an off-site for all first-line supervisors with special invitations to the General Supervisors to work on problems and socialize at the same time, anticipating that getting to know each other better might resolve some of the communication blocks.

Write down any other alternatives below:

_____

_____

_____

_____

Section Four
Communicating Effectively
Exercises and Case Histories
Related to
Chapter 7
Rules of Communication on the Gameboard

COMMUNICATION AND YOUR PLACE IN THE ORGANIZATION

Who do you talk to?
List all of the people you
ordinarily talk to during a
work week (you may list groups
of people with whom you meet as
individuals)

Why do you talk to them?
Describe why you talk to each
person or what you hope to
accomplish by talking:

1. _____ _____

2. _____ _____

3. _____ _____

4. _____ _____

5. _____ _____

6. _____ _____

7. _____ _____

8. _____ _____

9. _____ _____

Identify all of the people listed above in terms of their relationship to you at work:

(1) If superiors or subordinates, are they in your direct line of command, i.e., do you report to them or they to you? If they are somewhere in your line of command list them under "Direct Relationship," otherwise place them under "Indirect Relationship."

(2) If peers, are they people with whom you work closely, such as in the same function, unit, department or division? If so, list them under "Direct Relationship," otherwise place them under "Indirect Relationship."

	Direct Relationship	**Indirect Relationship**

Superiors:

_____	_____
_____	_____
_____	_____
_____	_____
_____	_____
_____	_____

Peers:

_____	_____
_____	_____
_____	_____
_____	_____
_____	_____
_____	_____

Subordinates:

_____	_____
_____	_____
_____	_____
_____	_____
_____	_____

Then, write a letter next to each name listed above to indicate your most common means of communicating with that person, according to the following scale:

    (A) Purposeful and task-centered
    (B) Supportive and responsive
    (C) Aggressive and controlling
    (D) Manipulative and coercive

Remember that purposeful and task-centered communication is appropriate when operating within an upright pyramid; supportive and responsive within a round circle; aggressive and controlling within a crooked pyramid; and manipulative and coercive within a squishy circle.

Now list below people you are not talking to or talking to frequently enough:

_____
_____
_____
_____
_____

List below the people with whom you talk more aggressively or manipulatively than purposefully or supportively:

_____
_____
_____
_____
_____

What steps can you take to improve your communication?

Section Five
Recognizing Group Rules
Exercises and Case Histories
Related to
Chapter 8
On Knowing the Unspoken Group Rules

ONCE I HAD AN IDEA . . .

Tom and two of his fellow supervisors from other areas decided to "walk in each other's shoes" for one day in order to understand the problems of each of the different areas. The three supervisors had difficulty setting up the specific day because of other demands, but finally settled on one day three weeks later. Tom suggested that they check their plan out with the plant manager. They made an appointment with the manager. At the time of the appointment, the plant manager was rushing between two other meetings. He heard them out, but said, "A lot is going on now, why don't you hold off for a while?" The next time they saw him in the hallway by the cafeteria. He looked at them briefly, said "Good idea, but not now." Tom and his fellows were discouraged and did not bring the idea up again.

How would Tom arrange to meet with the plant manager and what would he say at that meeting?

_____
_____
_____

Jack was a first-line supervisor who had an idea: he wanted to set up a series of meetings for other first-line supervisors so that they could agree on a list of questions which they wanted to ask their superiors about the plant's direction and the changing nature of their jobs. Jack asked those supervisors that he knew and they began to meet weekly. They drew up a list of questions and, in general, felt pleased with their progress. When Jack called the plant superintendent, he was greeted by an explosive: "What do you think you're doing?" It turned out, that some of the other supervisors who had not been invited to the meeting had talked with the superintendent at lunch and mentioned that a group of first-line people were meeting secretly to challenge management's direction.

What would Jack say to the superintendent in the remainder of the telephone call and the next time they meet?

_____
_____
_____

WHAT HAPPENED HERE?

In each of the situations described below, explain why the expected result was not achieved and what might have been done to achieve it.

In a certain assembly plant, Joe and other supervisors made a decision that *everybody* would wear safety glasses all the time from now on. Although this was a firm rule, people treated it casually and often did not bother with protective glasses. Joe and the supervisory group told their supervisors what they had decided, sent a letter announcing the importance of enforcing the old policy to all other supervisors, and made signs to put up about the plant letting the workers know about the importance of safety glasses. The week following this activity, Joe was pleased to note that his workers were all wearing safety glasses. The next week, however, as Joe went about the plant he saw that the workers in other departments were only sometimes wearing glasses. Many of them had their glasses stuck in their back pockets just as they used to do. Joe asked one or two supervisors what was going on and each of those supervisors shrugged and said that was the way it was . . . When Joe reported this back to the original supervisory group, several of *them* said, "Well, that's the way it is . . ."

What factors were operating in the plant which made it unlikely that Joe's plan would succeed?

_____

_____

_____

What specific actions might Joe have taken which would help his plan succeed?

_____

_____

_____

On the third shift of a components plant, one service department's supervisor met most requests and was generally well thought of in the plant. When this supervisor retired, Jeff, a new young supervisor, took his place. He was astonished to find that his workers took catnaps on the job - sometimes for an hour at a time. On his second week at work, he told his people firmly (he thought) that there would be no more sleeping on the job and that the department's goal was now to meet *all* requests promptly. The next night he sent an electrician to answer a call and found out four hours later that the electrician had idled an entire line by dismantling a working station. That same night there had been two fires in the plant and his workers said they were unable to prevent them or put them out without putting down two more lines. By the end of the month, Jeff's service record was the worst one in the maintenance area.

What factors were operating in this department which made it unlikely that Jeff would meet his goals?

_____
_____
_____

What might Jeff have done instead which would help him to achieve his goals?

_____
_____
_____

Rich was a "fast-tracker" in the education and training area who had a strong interest in creating new programs in human resource management. As part of his "career development" he was moved into a high-powered finance department in another city. He was given a few months to get his feet on the ground and then was asked to develop some new incentive programs and to suggest directions for new projects. His first two proposals were turned down abruptly and without explanation. Rich thought that they had merit and would motivate people as well as help the company. He realized that nobody else around there talked about "motivating people" and only about dollars and cents, but he was certain that his ideas would get a hearing. He worked harder on his next proposal, supporting it with some of the best evidence for the "human relations approach." This proposal was not only sent back to him immediately, he was issued a "friendly" reprimand by a senior person in the department who let him know that if he didn't change his ways his career would be in trouble.

What was Rich trying to achieve and why was it unlikely to be successful?

_____
_____
_____

What might Rich have done instead in order to achieve his goals?

_____
_____
_____

Mary started an employee involvement group in her department. She really believed that her employees could work together to solve some of the problems in the department. The initial group was excited about meeting and spent the first two or three sessions planning what they would do. Within a month or two, however, group members started missing meetings. When asked about their nonattendance, they said things like, "Well, we can't really do anything anyway. The group is only a gripe session." Finally, Mary asked them to take on responsibility for solving a specific problem. The group told her, in effect, "That's your job. Why do you want us to do it for you?"

What group rules were in existence that made it difficult for Mary to establish a real problem-solving group?

_____
_____
_____

What might she have done to better achieve her goals for the group?

_____
_____
_____

What group rules are operating in your work setting which at least sometimes make it difficult for you to achieve your goals?

_____
_____
_____
_____
_____

Are there ways that you might change these group rules or expectations?

Section Six
Planning for Oneself and the Organization

Exercises and Case Histories
Related to
Chapter 9
Managing the Change Process

WORKING UNDER FIRE

Marjorie P. was a first-line supervisor in a manufacturing plant. She had 28 employees working for her. She complained often that she never had time to breath from the time she got to work in the morning until she left for home at night. Friday, June 3, was a typical day. Marjorie arrived at work at 7:30 AM. She met with the supervisor of the night shift and was told of the problems with two machines that had occurred just before her arrival. In order for her unit to stay on schedule, she would have to get the machines working immediately. At her station, she had a note from the Committeeman wanting to talk with her about an employee she had recently threatened to write up. Before she had time to deal with either of these concerns, she remembered a meeting with her supervisor at 8:00 AM. She rushed off to the meeting and heard, along with her co-workers, that they would have to figure out a way to maintain their current production with 1/6 less of the work force for the next two months. The economic picture required more layoffs. As she emerged from the meeting she saw two of her workers engaged in an argument over a procedural matter. She stopped to talk with them and worked things through. This took half an hour. As she made her way back to her station, another employee stopped her. This woman was nearly in tears about some difficulties she was having with other workers. Marjorie sat down with her for over half an hour and then they went to see her supervisor. It was 10:30 before Marjorie returned to her station and found that the necessary parts for her department had not yet arrived. In addition, she was faced with the problems presented by the machinery and the Committeeman. Her workers were all restless and annoyed because the machines were down. "Have you called maintenance yet?" they asked. "Called maintenance!" she replied, reaching for the phone, "when would I do that?" Half an hour later, Marjorie slumped down at the coffee table with her usual midmorning headache and said, "Does it always have to be this way?"

Rank Marjorie's activities in the order of their importance - as you see it. Which activities should she have attended to first? Which last? What else should she have done during the morning? Then write a new schedule for her morning that would fit with the rankings you have assigned.

A. Place a 1 in front of the most important activity and continue with a 2, 3 and so forth until you finish the list:

___ Getting machines fixed
___ Talking to the Committeeman
___ One-hour supervisory meeting
___ Employee argument
___ Personal problem of employee
___ Chasing parts
___ Other _____

B. Write a schedule of how Marjorie might have most effectively spent her morning:

7:30 AM_____
8:00 AM_____
8:30 AM_____
9:00 AM_____
9:30 AM_____
10:00 AM_____
10:30 AM_____

ESTABLISHING SUPERVISORY PRIORITIES

1. In the appropriate columns below, list (a) all the activities you generally do during an ordinary workday, (b) those additional activities you do about once a week, and (c) those you do about once a month.

(a) Daily activities	(b) Weekly activities
_____	_____
_____	_____
_____	_____
_____	_____
_____	_____
_____	**(c) Monthly activities**
_____	_____
_____	_____
_____	_____

_____   _____
_____   _____
_____   _____

2. Place an asterisk next to the three most important daily activities and one or two of the most important weekly and monthly activitites.

3. How much time (in hours and minutes) do you spend in the three most important daily activities?_____ Multiply this number by five to arrive at number of hours per week:_____ How much time do you spend in your most important weekly activities? _____ How much time in your most important monthly activities _____ Divide this number by four to arrive at approximate number of hours per week:_____ Now add up the number of hours per week that you spend in important activities and write this number here: _____ Is this number greater than or less than 40? _____ Do you need more time for these important activities or is your time sufficient?__

4. If you are spending too little time in high priority activities (or if you would like to increase the time spent in these activities) examine your list of low-priority items (anything which you did not mark with an asterisk).

    Are there any items on the list which could be done by somebody else so that you could delegate responsibility for these activities? If so, list these activities:

    _____   _____
    _____   _____
    _____   _____

    Are there any items which could be omitted or done less often without any loss in job performance? List these activities:

    _____   _____

    Are there any activities which would take less time if they were handled differently? That is, would advance planning, scheduling, or development of routine procedures simplify this activity and decrease the amount of time required to do it? List the activity and the steps that you might take to handle this differently:

_____
_____
_____
_____

If you were to do all these things, how much time per week could you devote to high priority items that you are spending otherwise now? _

5. Do you think it is practical/realistic to do any of these things? Which ones? When?

WORTHWHILE GOALS & REALISTIC PROJECTS

Decide on at least three worthwhile, i.e. significant, goals which you believe would better your organization if achieved:

_____
_____
_____

Take one of these goals and write down all the steps that would have to be taken to achieve this goal at several levels. Continue to do this until you individually have identified one thing you might realistically do to work toward this goal. Be sure you can identify the people, resources, and time with which you could do this. Then list what you might do as a realistic project.

WORTHWHILE GOAL:_____

STEPS: _____
                _____
                _____
                _____
                _____

_____

_____

_____

_____

_____

_____

REALISTIC PROJECT:_____

■■

THINGS I HAVE DONE & THINGS I HOPE TO DO

List three things you have accomplished in your career and identify the larger more significant goal which your work helped to achieve:

Accomplishment	Significance
_____	_____
_____	_____
_____	_____

List one to three things you hope to accomplish in the next several years and identify the larger more significant goals which your work would help to achieve:

Accomplishment	Significance
_____	_____
_____	_____
_____	_____

Do you have a plan for accomplishing these tasks? Are you going to start working toward these goals? Now? Later? Why?

Section Seven
Organizational Change &
Management Decisions

Exercises and Case Histories
Related to
Chapter 10
Playing the Game with Changing Rules

SUPERVISION IN TIMES OF CHANGE

Ed was plant manager of a manufacturing facility. His division had established guidelines which required that each unit meet higher standards for quality and at the same time increase production by 10%. At the same time, due to a difficult economic situation, overall costs were to be decreased by 10%. Ed's success in achieving these goals would be monitored on the next four quarterly reports and reflected in his annual performance review.

Several alternatives are open to him:

(1) He may require closer supervision of his employees and "force" the 10% increase out of them. At the same time he may further limit inventories and require a reduction in scrap in order to cut the cost of supplies. Employees who continue to maintain high scrap rates will be disciplined.

(2) He may ask his employees for suggestions on improving profit in one-to-one conversations and in group meetings and recommend discontinuation of projects where increased profit is not possible.

(3) He may introduce training programs which increase employee interpersonal skills so that they work more effectively together. At the same time he may give them training in labor relations so that they work more effectively with the union in setting high standards for employees.

(4) He may recommend investment in ten new machines to improve quality and efficiency and, at the same time, make plans for downsizing the labor force as the computerized equipment cuts down process time for each part.

(5) He may establish meetings for employees to set up and monitor their own schedules, believing that they would then work more effectively. At the same time he would encourage employees to set standards for performance designate low-performing employees for training or discipline.

(6) He may arrange meetings to develop a better interface with the maintenance operation so that machines are repaired more quickly and there is less down time, believing that a new cooperation among functions would both improve productivity and quality and cut costs.

If you were Ed, which alternative of those above would you choose? If you prefer a different combination of the above alternatives or another altogether, write down your choice below:

_____
_____
_____

Describe how implementation of your alternative would affect costs, productivity and morale for each quarter of the coming year.

Section Eight
The Life of Paul Z.

Exercises and Case Histories
Related to
Chapter 11
Learning and Growing and Winning the Game

RUNNING ON THE FAST TRACK

The following is a list of events from the life of Paul Z.:

1959   Graduated from high school
          Hired as hourly production worker for Aircraft, Inc.

1960   Laid off for 6 months

1961   Cited for disorderly conduct: case dismissed

1962   Local bowling league champion
          Hand injured in hunting accident
          Excellent performance appraisal & bonus
          "Production Worker of the Year"

1963   Moved in with Marilyn P.
          Totalled car on ski trip
          Lost driver's license for too many points
          Medical leave
          Hired as first-line supervisor at Automobile, Inc.

1964   Broke up with Marilyn P.
          Cited for disorderly conduct: $750 fine
          "Best Poker Player in Plant 5"
          Married Donna C.

1965   First child, Bobby born

1966   Second child, Tommy, born
          Bought house

1969   Bobby hit by car, lapses into coma, & dies
          Donna was depressed & took Tommy to live with her parents
          Highest production record in five plants
          Donna returned home to Paul with Tommy
          [Paul] accepted responsibility for 1/2 of child care

1970 Began night school 3 times a week
Father died
Mother moved in
Mother had stroke and went to nursing home
Donna took Tommy and went back to her parents
Rented house and moved into apartment

1974 Promoted to Assistant Superintendent
Divorce from Donna final
Met Carol T., divorced woman with three children

1976 Completed night school
Moved in with Carol
Mother died
Commended for excellence in supervision

1977 Plant Superintendent retired
Carol threatened to leave if marriage not forthcoming
Began graduate program at night
. . . . ? ? ? ? ? ? ?

Check the items which you believe are likely to occur in Paul Z.'s life in the next five years?

___ Marriage   ___ Medical leave
___ Divorce   ___ Drinks too much
___ Another child   ___ Heart attack
___ Completes MBA   ___ Very early retirement
___ Becomes plant superintendent   ___ Lateral transfer
___ Sent to Advanced Management ___ Leaves Carol
   Training   ___ Killed in hunting accident
___ Coaches high school football   ___ Loses mortgage payment
___ Other?_____   playing poker

Write a story for the years 1977-1982 of Paul's life. Explain why you think your version of Paul's life is a likely story.

MANAGEMENT AND LEADERSHIP

The year was 1984. Paul Z. was plant superintendent of a manufacturing facility. At this moment, he was sitting in his office reviewing the last six years. During that time he had been promoted to his present job. A lateral move to a larger plant have been offered to him two years ago but he had turned down the offer to stay in the same geographic location. Together, he and Carol had five children, four from their previous marriages and one from their own marriage. At some time, all of the children had been living with them and there were three at home now. One of Carol's girls had been seriously ill and would always remain slightly weak and in need of physical therapy. The youngest child, a boy, seemed to be exceptionally bright and was in a special program in the local school system. Paul sometimes wondered if his reasons for not taking the other job were excuses or *real* reasons. Now was one of those times.

When Paul had made the commitment to stay with his home plant, he had poured his energies into new projects, determined to make this the best plant possible. He spent lots of time on the floor and avoided going to what he regarded as unnecessary meetings. He encouraged all his supervisors to try out new ideas and to experiment with cost efficient methods. Some of the results had been surprising. One department had painted its machines different colors and productivity went up. Workers in all departments were then allowed to have coffee near their stations. Productivity went up again. All departments also placed charts at the end of each line which displayed in big numbers the quantity of parts turned out by each shift. Productivity increased again. Finally, the maintenance people had worked out a decent computer dispatch system and everyone was spending less time with "down" machines. All in all it had been a very good period of time.

Some of the other plants which were closely related to Paul's had not, however, welcomed the changes in Paul's plant. Men from the other plants said that all these changes were a passing fad and would fade away with time. Many of these men were friends with the workers in Paul's plant . . . and sometimes Paul's own workers acted as if they didn't believe that all these changes were to be taken seriously. They expected that any day now Paul would return to "kicking ass" and give up the fancy trimmings.

Later that month, it looked as if that time had come. It had been a hectic week and new orders had come in with a priority stamp putting regular production behind schedule. Visitors from foreign plants had also taken up the regular production time. When it became clear that schedules were down, Paul called a meeting of his five General Supervisors. Actually only two Generals were notified of the meeting and arrived to find no one else there. Paul himself was late. Both Generals were angry about being taken away from the floor at such a hectic time when it appeared there would be no meeting after all. As they grumbled to the secretary Paul rushed in, postponed the Generals' meeting, and set a new meeting time with his secretary and told her sternly, **"Notify everyone,** this time!"

As Paul was talking with his secretary, one of the Generals who had just left stomped back into the office with a supervisor and two hourlies in tow. While the General had been at the "non-meeting", one of the hourlies had started shoving the other one, who had responded by throwing a tool at the first one. The tool missed and landed in one of the machines, causing that machine to grind to a halt which brought down the rest of the line. The first-line supervisor happening on this incident had begun yelling at the two men who were grappling with each other. The supervisor had pulled them apart physically. One of them had then had called his Committeeman. The General Supervisor, Tom, said "See, what happens when you let this plant run itself! We've always said it was a mistake."

While the situation was being explained to Paul, a crowd of workers, including some supervisors, was hanging around outside the office waiting to see what would happen. Tom was shifting from one foot to the other uncomfortably and the supervisor and two workers looked angry. "Go on back to work," Paul said firmly to the onlookers and they began to disperse. "Maybe," said one supervisor in the crowd, "he'll finally start kicking ass around here and everything will get back to normal." Paul glanced at the back of the departing workers and supervisors but said nothing. He turned to Tom and said:

_____

_____

_____

What did Paul say?

Rank the following alternatives in the order of your preference with 1 being high and 6 being low:

a. ___ Get the Committeeman in here. We'll find out who started this and let's write it up.

b. ___ I want you four guys to talk this over among yourselves and come to a solution quick. I want you not only to tell me what to do with you but how we are going to communicate this to the rest of them out there.

c. ___ Go on back to work but don't let this happen again. The next time you will be removed from the floor.

d. ___ Let's sit down and talk this out together and see what the real problem is.

e. ___ "Kicking ass" is really what the game is about after all. The two of you are laid off, effective today, and both supervisors are temporarily demoted.

f. ___ I want to break up this bunch of rowdies. Immediate transfers will be forthcoming for all of you.

If you have another alternative, write it down below:

_____

_____

_____

Justify your answers in terms of choosing the "most effective management processes."

SUCCEEDING IN TIMES OF CHANGE

It was late afternoon one Friday in the fall of 1985. Paul Z. was sitting at his desk in the plant staring at the wall. He shook his head slightly and looked around his office at the papers and books strewn across his desk. "Usually," he thought, "I feel pretty good on Friday knowing that a lot of things have got done and other things are in the works. In the last two years, I've often gone home with a sense of accomplishment. Today, I don't feel like that. I feel a little uneasy. I wonder why."

Paul sat at his desk and reviewed what had happened that afternoon.

Several people had talked to him about their work and their problems. This was not unusual. Maybe it was something they had said that was bothering him. He went back in his mind over the afternoon's conversations.

George was the first to come in. He'd started some new group projects in his area and one group of employees had had several sucesses. Now he was concerned that this group was losing its motivation. Lately they kept comparing themselves with the men in the next department who *didn't* work all the time but goofed off and read newspapers. If the supervisor of the other area didn't straighten up his area, George thought his own people were going to slack off and lose interest in keeping their projects going. As George had talked about his department his shoulders had drooped forward slightly and his mouth appeared to turn downward.

Suzanne had called him on the phone after George had left. She was taking over a new department which was made up of a lot of people brought in from other areas which had been temporarily closed down. She said she was challenged by the new assignment but her voice was higher than usual and just a little squeaky. Her voice conveyed her nervousness about her new assignment.

Douglas had spoken to him briefly when he stopped in the cafeteria for coffee in the midafternoon. Doug was confused about the definition of his job. He said there were so many changes in the plant lately that he didn't even know who his boss was. New teams had been created recently and the supervisors reported to new people. Sometimes this was not at all clear to the supervisors. Moreover, Doug didn't know if it was his job to go to meetings or his job to be on the floor with his workers. He left saying, "What does a supervisor do anyway?"

After leaving the cafeteria, Paul had gone to a meeting where he had a chance to talk briefly with Tom. For two years, he had worked closely with Tom and together they had done a good job of running the plant. Tom, however, had recently become more involved with quality control and had been chiefly responsible for implementing a computerized quality control system which had already saved the plant thousands of dollars. Because of his success, Tom had been transferred to the nearby plant to help them implement the same system. Just before the meeting got underway, however, Tom told Paul that the funds for the system at the other plant had been put on hold and he wasn't sure whether the system was "go" or not. He tapped his pencil rapidly on the table as he said this - just as the meeting was called to order.

Paul had left the meeting with John who had recently been promoted to Superintendent of another plant. As John had headed for the parking lot, he slapped Paul on the back and said, "Well, I guess we both know the ropes around here. Sometimes you just have to agree with the powers that be. You've always done a good job of that, Paul."

As Paul thought this over, he realized that all these people were sharing with him a feeling of uncertainty about their jobs. Somehow he had picked this up and now he felt uncertain about his job! Was he doing the right thing to stay where he was? Should he be interested in moving up? Was moving up the same thing as "being a politician?" Paul shook his head, picked up his coat, and went out the door, shutting it with a bang.

On a scale from 1 to 10 (1 is low and 10 is high) estimate the degree of uncertainty which you believe each individual was experiencing on that Friday afternoon:

Paul	___	George	___
Suzanne	___	Douglas	___
Tom	___	John	___

On a scale from 1 to 10 (1 is low and 10 is high) estimate the degree of comfort which you would experience if *you* were in the situation described:

Paul	___	George	___
Suzanne	___	Douglas	___
Tom	___	John	___

Then formulate one piece of advice for each individual. This advice could be in the form of a phrase, or a picture, or a symbol. What do you think is the most constructive thing you could say to each person?

Answers and Commentaries

IDENTIFYING PERSONALITY PATTERNS (p. 202)

John is most likely a **Producer**
Allen is most likely a **Processor**
Arthur is most likely a **Producer**
Tom is most likely an **Integrator**
Alice is most likely a **Producer**

[Three of these characters are fictionalized versions of individuals with whom we worked at Ford Motor Company in 1981-1982 and two represent individuals whom we met in initial assessment situations at Rochester Products in 1982.]

PERSONALITY PATTERNS IN INTERACTION (p. 204)

Tom would most likely be disappointed in John's and Alice's work in areas (d), (e), and (f). Allen would be most likely to identify technical competence as (a), (d) and (f). Arthur would be most likely to identify technical competence as (b), (c) and (e).

[These characters and statements were drawn primarily from actual events and conversations at Ford Motor Company in 1981. The discussion of technical competence reflects a real conversation between Allen and Arthur during that period of time. Since that time Allen and Arthur have agreed to disagree and in the process Allen has become something of a mentor to Arthur. It was important to clarify the differences which existed, however, before the two men could reach an accord.]

RESOLVING PERSONALITY CONFLICTS (p. 205)

Bobby is probably a **Processor**
Susan is most likely an **Integrator** or maybe a **Producer**
Jack is probably an **Integrator**
Bobby's main strength lies in his **inventiveness**
Susan's main strength lies in her **ability to organize** and **to get the work done**

Harry has a variety of alternatives in this situation: he may ask them to recognize and tolerate their differences, he may emphasize the need to work together toward the goal regardless of differences, he may suggest that Susan and Bobby meet with him to develop a strategy so that both can do what they do best without interference from the other. In the long-term a recognition and respect for differences will lead to a greater accord between the two contending individuals.

In terms of meeting short-term goals, however, Harry probably has to mandate that both will return to work, put personal feelings and preferences aside, and get the job done. A set time to resolve differences, and a commitment to do so, however, will make it easier for the two to meet the short-term goal.

The viability of your solution depends on how well you know yourself and the situations which come to your mind as you read the story. A variety of solutions are possible - but depend on knowledge of self, others and the situation as a whole. How you explain your decision is perhaps more important than the decision itself.

WORKING FROM STRENGTH (p. 208)

This exercise is designed to have you evaluate your strengths as determined by the PXI and then establish your own list of strengths. You are always a better judge of yourself than a paper-and-pencil inventory. However, the inventory is very useful in asking you to look at yourself more closely and giving you a new perspective on your own behavior. The remaining sections of the exercise are asking you to explore your own characteristics in terms of your current and desired job position.

I GOTTA BE TOUGH (p. 212)

In all of these exercises, drawn from real management situations, it is possible to justify almost any answer depending on how you view your own strengths, the capabilities of others with whom you work, and the situation as a whole. The most commonly chosen answers, by managers, are (e) and (f) backed up by (b), (c) or (d) depending on how those responding interpreted the situation.

[This story is drawn from that of a manager at Ford Motor Company who experienced many of these difficulties in gaining acceptance from others of his new behavior. His choice in this situation was (e) to go to the work groups, establish good relationships with the men on the floor, and work toward creating better communication channels from the floor up. This approach worked for him since his supervisors were stronger than he in the eyes of the workers and inclined very nicely to shut him out. Having the support of the men (who also supported the supervisors) gave him the leverage to effectively use alternative (c) and work through difficulties on a one-to-one basis with the supervisors.]

WHO'S TO BLAME? (p. 216)

Again, the most frequently chosen alternatives were (e) and (f) backed up by (b) and (c).

[In the actual situation, however, taken from an event occurring at Rochester Products during one of our early visits there, this supervisor used (b), (c) and (d). None of these was particularly effective and a later analysis of his work strengths showed that he was better suited to a more technical job; he was transferred to such a position and soon was pleased with his work and his productivity.]

Chief: (a)
Patriarch: (d)
Counselor: (c)
Facilitator: (e)
Role Model: (b)
Team Leader: (f)

WHATEVER IT TAKES (p. 218)

The most commonly chosen alternatives for Tom's dilemma are (e) and (f) generally backed up by (d) because the number of workers makes (c) an unlikely possibility. A frequently chosen variation of (c) was to speak with a selected number of workers, both those who could help Tom because of their own strength at work, and, later, those who might be specifically causing difficulties in meeting schedules.

[This situation was drawn from initial interviews at a different facility (from that referred to above) in Rochester Products. The difficulties which Tom incurred eventually led to his leaving the supervisory ranks. The lists of alternatives reflect mostly positive alternatives which Tom might have tried -- but he did not do so.]

NOBODY TELLS US ANYTHING (p. 219)

Answers to this problem situation were variable and depended greatly upon how one saw the situation, the nature of one's boss and the support or non-support of other supervisors. A large number of respondents to this story, however, began with (b) and moved to (d). Actual supervisors were sensitive about talking opening with many other supervisors but did suggest that they might talk with one or two in order to get information -- sometimes as a first priority.

[Mark worked in the same plant as Tom and his story again was one that we heard on initial interviews in the facility. Mark's initial response to the real situation was (a) but he was later in a situation in which he could use (b) comfortably and ask his boss for information. He was also aware that he needed more contact with other supervisors and began to establish stronger peer relationships where he found both support and information.]

COMMUNICATION AND YOUR PLACE IN THE ORGANIZATION (p. 224)

This exercise is designed to assist you in examining your communication patterns at work, to identify the purpose of your communications, and how well you achieve those purposes. Once you have analyzed these patterns, you may see some directions in which you want to improve your communication with others.

ONCE I HAD AN IDEA (p. 228)

Both of these incidents are similar to actual projects undertaken by supervisors and managers at Rochester Products which were never satisfactorily completed. In fictionalizing these accounts, managers were asked to distance themselves from the actual event and create a strategy for achieving their goals. A series of responses, each of which might be best given the particular situation, follow:

Tom might:
> Establish a new meeting time with the manager
> Talk with one of the lieutenants of the manager first
> Give the manager something succinct in writing which might elicit a quick response
> Draw support from many other supervisors so that a group meeting might be requested with -- and honored by -- the

manager
Undertake a very small part of the plan without approval -- and
in no way that the manager might object to -- in order to have
initial evidence of success in a pilot venture
Prepare for any meeting thoroughly with documentation of the
breadth and depth of support
Develop figures which show how the costs of operating the
plant might be significantly cut by instituting such a procedure
. . . and so forth

The point is that if you have a good idea it probably can be implemented if
you are willing to do your homework, acquire support from your peers, and
choose an appropriate way and time in which to see your boss. Many
answers might lead to a solution depending on the situation.

Jack might:
Apologize to his boss for not talking about this with him earlier
Furnish his boss with minutes or notes from the meetings
Ask his boss to meet with the group of supervisors and give
them his suggestions
Offer to send the boss full accountings of any future meetings

All of these are steps which diffuse some of the negative effect of not having
informed the boss earlier of the meetings so that he would not be taken by
surprise - and including him to any extent he wishes in any future meetings.
In most cases, the boss will then agree to the continuation of the project -
at least after his viewpoint has been taken into account. If management is
really opposed to supervisors meeting with each other, then another strategy
would have to be enacted.

WHAT HAPPENED HERE? (p. 229)

Each exercise was designed to elicit the *unspoken group rules* which had
hindered - or might hinder - the successful accomplishment of a supervisory
or managerial goal. Any listing of responses would be lengthy so a few
sample responses will be given for each situation.

In Joe's case existence of the following unspoken rules might make it unlikely that he would succeed:

> **Nobody really cares if glasses are worn or not**
> **Wearing glasses is not a cool thing to do**
> **It's not good to stand out from the group**
> **It's important not to go along with the supervisors too much**

What might Joe do to help his plan succeed?

> **Get the workers to buy into the idea by use of dramatic films, by rewarding workers who wear glasses in a way which doesn't separate them from their group, or, perhaps most importantly, by asking them to help formulate the initial plan . . .**

In Jeff's case existence of the following unspoken rules might make it unlikely that he would succeed:

> **Sleeping on the night shift is at least OK and maybe cool**
> **New supervisors don't know much**
> **The workers really control what happens . . .**

What might Jeff do to help him succeed?

> **Get to know the men and the area before making new rules**
> **Show respect for the former supervisor**
> **Respect the knowledge of the men**
> **Ask the men to tell him what they want to see changed**

In Rich's case existence of the following unspoken rule might make it unlikely that he would succeed:

> **All good proposals are quantitative and/or financial**
> **New guys don't know much**
> **Human relations stuff doesn't work . . .**

What might Rich do to help him succeed?
> **Ask the advice of his seniors**
> **Learn to see things from a financial viewpoint**
> **Phrase his proposals in quantitative terms**

Get external advice and documentation on a variety of incentive programs and offer those more senior than he a choice in selecting the approach

In Mary's case existence of the following unspoken group rules might make it unlikely that she would succeed:

Workers can't really change anything
Supervisors do their job and we do ours
Allowing workers to do what they want to do is a sign of supervisory weakness . . .

What might Mary do to help her succeed?

Provide sufficient structure and guidance to help the group have success in initial problem-solving sessions
Discontinue any meetings of the group which degenerate into gripe sessions
Provide training for her workers in leading problem-solving groups
Make clear the overall goals of the group and reward workers for taking steps toward accomplishing them

[Most but not all of the following situations also reflected real events at Rochester Products Division.]

<hr>

WORKING UNDER FIRE (p. 234)

Many supervisors had a similar list of responses to Marjorie's problems which involved planning ahead (sometimes coming in early), delegating tasks and postponing less critical matters for later in the day. A typical response would be (1) get in line to get the machines fixed by calling maintenance; (2) make an appointment with the Committeeman at a later time; (3) have one of her lead workers track down the parts; (4) attend the meeting (even if slightly late); (5) schedule a later appointment for the two workers in difficulty, (6) take the time immediately for the upset employee; amd (7) after coffee, she would check to make sure the machines were fixed and lines were up, then (8) sit down with the two workers and (9) meet with the Committeeman.

The remaining exercises in Section Five are self-explanatory.

SUPERVISION IN TIMES OF CHANGE (p. 240)

All of the "best" plans combined part of several of the different listed alternatives and then made a good case for a decrease in costs and increase in productivity and morale over the year. The clarity of projected consequences, and accompanying explanation, was more critical than the actual choices in preparing plans which might be workable.

RUNNING ON THE FAST TRACK (p. 244)

Any particular sequence of events would be a defensible response in this case history. More interesting, what do your responses reflect in your own attitudes toward change? Does a difficult period in life necessarily forecast later troubles? How related are work and family histories in your own mind? Where do you place your priorities? Does Paul face problems or opportunities? What is the difference?

MANAGEMENT AND LEADERSHIP (p. 246)

The best solutions to this situation were created by the managers and supervisors who studied this story - and took account of the short-term crisis and long-term development so that such crises were less likely to occur again. In the short-term, workers were sent back to work, at the same time as long-term issues were confronted by establishing various types of group meetings with the goal of educating everyone about the direction of the plant and ultimately letting them have a voice in establishing that direction. The frequent response of "sitting down and talking about this" in various forms all proved unworkable on closer examination.

SUCCEEDING IN TIMES OF CHANGE (p. 248)

All the advice offered by managers and supervisors to Paul and his people generally emphasized the importance of standing back from the situation, not making "mountains out of molehills," and staying grounded in one's own perception of oneself and one's job. In general, in many different forms, managers and supervisors said not to make decisions after a long day or one unhappy experience. The individual takes a long-term view and accepts the chaff along with the wheat . . .

Index

About the Author

Barbara E. Kovach, Ph.D. is Director of the Leadership Development Institute and Professor of Management and Psychology at Rutgers University. Formerly, she served as Dean of University College at Rutgers (1984-1988) and was Professor of Psychology and Chair of the Department of Behavioral Sciences at the University of Michigan - Dearborn (1973-1984). She received her Ph.D. from the University of Maryland and her B.A. and M.A. from Stanford University.

As president and co-founder of Human Systems Analysis, Inc., she was a long-term consultant for Rochester Products Division of General Motors (1982-1987), and worked with divisions of Ford Motor Company (1981-1982) and AT&T (1982-1983). Her books include **Outsiders on the Inside, Power and Love, Organizational Sync, The Flexible Organization** and **Survival on the Fast Track.** She is a frequent speaker for academic and corporate audiences.

Dr. Kovach and her husband have three children and live in Princeton.